D1551617

Mind, Machine, and Metaphor

New Perspectives on Law, Culture, and Society

Robert W. Gordon and Margaret Jane Radin,
Series Editors

*Mind, Machine, and Metaphor: An Essay on Artificial Intelligence
and Legal Reasoning,* Alexander E. Silverman

*Rebellious Lawyering: One Chicano's Vision of Progressive
Law Practice,* Gerald P. López

Wittgenstein and Legal Theory,
edited by Dennis M. Patterson

Pragmatism in Law and Society,
edited by Michael Brint and William Weaver

Feminist Legal Theory: Readings in Law and Gender,
edited by Katharine T. Bartlett and Rosanne Kennedy

FORTHCOMING

*Words That Wound: Critical Race Theory, Assaultive Speech,
and the First Amendment,* Mari J. Matsuda, Charles R. Lawrence III,
Richard Delgado, and Kimberlè Williams Crenshaw

Intellect and Craft: Writings of Justice Hans Linde,
edited by Robert F. Nagel

*Property and Persuasion: Normativity and Change
in the Jurisprudence of Property,* Carol M. Rose

*Failed Revolutions: Why Good Intentions, Great Promise,
and Boundless Energy Fail to Transform the World,*
Richard Delgado and Jean Stefancic

The Philosophy of International Law: A Human Rights Approach,
Fernando R. Tesón

*In Whose Name? Feminist Legal Theory and
the Experience of Women,* Christine A. Littleton

Mind, Machine, and Metaphor

An Essay on Artificial Intelligence and Legal Reasoning

Alexander E. Silverman

Westview Press

BOULDER • SAN FRANCISCO • OXFORD

New Perspectives on Law, Culture, and Society

Copyright © 1993 by Alexander E. Silverman

Published in 1993 in the United States of America by Westview Press, Inc., 5500 Central Avenue, Boulder, Colorado 80301-2877, and in the United Kingdom by Westview Press, 36 Lonsdale Road, Summertown, Oxford OX2 7EW

A CIP catalog record for this book is available from the Library of Congress.
ISBN 0-8133-8575-X

Printed and bound in the United States of America

The paper used in this publication meets the requirements
of the American National Standard for Permanence of Paper
for Printed Library Materials Z39.48-1984.

10   9   8   7   6   5   4   3   2   1

To Jared, for asking why the birds fly south

Contents

Preface and Acknowledgments   xi

1   Introduction   1

2   Artificial Intelligence and . . .   3

3   Simulated Vehicles in the Park   35

4   Paradigm Shifts   59

5   Law as Mind-Machine   77

6   Rules and Judgment   89

7   A Final Word   109

Appendix   111
Notes   115
Bibliography   133
About the Book and Author   145

Preface and Acknowledgments

The word "essay" in this book's subtitle was chosen deliberately. The book raises many questions that it does not answer and treats in a preliminary or speculative fashion subject areas that might be explored further in a longer work. Several readers of early drafts offered excellent suggestions for ways that the book could be expanded in scope and depth. However, in view of the time that would be required to respond fully to these suggestions, and the rapidity with which artificial intelligence technology is changing, it seemed best to publish the book in its current form. I hope that readers will find the ideas presented here to be helpful, fun, and worth pursuing.

I am indebted to Ruth Adams, Jay Atlas, Mark Berlin, Patrick Castelaz, David Chapman, Tom Grey, J. B. Kennedy, Derek Koehler, George Lakoff, Mari Matsuda, Helen Nissenbaum, Richard Perry, David Rosenhan, David Rumelhart, Paul Thagard, Robert Weisberg, and Steven Winter for their support, encouragement, and valuable insights. I was introduced to the idea of connectionist networks as function construction machines in a lecture by Thomas Caudell in Caudell's course Introduction to Artificial Neural Systems, taught at UCLA Extension, Spring 1988. Thanks to Laura Yedwab for the streetlight example in Chapter 3, and to Susan Palwick for the grocery-shopping metaphor in Chapter 4. Special thanks to my advisers Peggy Radin and Dean Schlobohm; to Daniel Weise, who introduced me to interactionism and gave me detailed feedback on an early draft of Chapter 2; and to Gustav Larsson, who furnished the town square example in Chapter 3 and who listened for hours to my half-formed ideas as they were taking shape. This book would not have been completed without the help of Spencer Carr and Shena Redmond, my editors at Westview, and Renée Glover, who provided me with access to a laser printer when I most needed one.

Thanks most of all to Susie Skadron, for faithful love and patience.

Alexander E. Silverman

1

Introduction

People write about artificial intelligence (AI) and law from any of several viewpoints. They may write as computer scientists, describing the development and implementation of a legal expert system or similar computer program, often in considerable technical detail. They may write as practicing attorneys, discussing the application of particular computer programs or systems in actual law practice. They may write as commentators on legal doctrine relating to AI, especially intellectual property law. Finally, they may write as legal theorists, speculating on the jurisprudential implications of AI.

This essay takes the legal theorist's viewpoint. Attempts to apply so-called classical AI approaches to legal problem solving have met with limited success. Classical AI approaches embody brittle models of law and of human reasoning, and the limitations of these approaches are in essence the limitations of their models. Legal theorists and jurists often subscribe to the same sorts of models and encounter the same sorts of problems. New directions in AI research solve some of the problems of the classical approaches while raising new issues of their own. These new directions can illuminate new directions for jurisprudence as well.

The essay's organization is as follows: Chapter 2 is an overview of AI technology, focusing on issues relevant to later discussion. Also included is a discussion of legal expert systems and an introduction to the mind-machine metaphor. In Chapter 3 I use the well-known vehicle-in-the-park problem to illustrate the limits of classical AI and to develop concepts of indeterminacy, open texture, and essential vagueness. The centrality of the categorization problem to AI and to legal reasoning is discussed. Chapter 4 is an exploration of whether the concept of Kuhnian paradigm shifts has meaning in AI and law or, for that matter, in science. Discussions of legal pragmatism and the nature of theory set the framework for the analysis. In Chapter 5 new metaphors of law are developed, the most important being that of law as connectionist AI system embodied in society. The entailments of the metaphors are considered; in particular, legal rules are seen as best-fit approximations to the law. In Chapter 6 I focus on what the AI-law analogy suggests about human legal reasoning. The notion of the rule of law as something other than the law of rules is suggested, and the relationship between judicial opinion writing and human explanation capability is considered.

This essay takes seriously the notion that metaphor, rather than being mere trope, is essential to human thought and language, and in particular to the process of jurisprudential theory-building. Changes in theory are linked to changes in conceptual or metaphorical framework. In developing new metaphors of law, this essay does not purport to describe what law *is*. Rather, it illustrates how law may be *seen* in new and potentially useful ways.

Thomas Grey writes that theory is good for getting us out of trouble as we attempt to solve problems. He goes on to note that theory can also be a medium of play—deep play, but play nonetheless.[1] It may well be that this or any jurisprudential essay is no more (or less) than a game. On the other hand, sometimes playing a game can be therapeutic.

2

Artificial Intelligence and . . .

There is such a thing [as human nature], *and it is not entirely tractable.*
—Melvin Konner, *The Tangled Wing* (1982)

Approaches to AI

Roughly speaking, AI is the attempt by computer scientists to model or simulate intelligent behavior on computers. An overview of the field is beyond the scope of this essay, but it is helpful to review some concepts that will be important later on. The *classical* and *connectionist* approaches, which compose the mainstream of AI research, are discussed in this section, along with the newer *fuzzy* approaches. (The more radical *interactionist* approaches are taken up in the last section of the chapter.)[1]

Classical and Connectionist Approaches

AI researchers have adopted two main sets, or families, of approaches, the classical and the connectionist approaches. Classical approaches include rule-based expert systems, frame systems, blackboard systems, logic programming, and various other related approaches. They served as the basis of the vast majority of AI research from the early 1960s through the mid-1980s and continue to serve as the basis for most AI research today. Connectionist approaches, also called parallel distributed processing or artificial neural network approaches, attempt to model or to pattern themselves after the processing mechanisms of human and animal brains. Examples include backpropagation networks, Hopfield networks, and adaptive resonance models. Connectionist approaches were first tried as early as the 1940s but nearly died out in the late 1960s. They have enjoyed a resurgence within the past decade and, according to their proponents, have provided useful methods for solving certain problems that had been difficult or intractable under classical approaches.[2]

The various classical approaches, although dissimilar in many respects, share a great deal in common with one another. Classical AI systems are written in programming languages such as LISP, PROLOG, or variants of these. Typically they express information as verbal statements or lists of word-like symbols, e.g., DOG, CAT, VEHICLE; such symbols represent the most primitive level of information in the system and are not "understood" by the computer except as they relate to other such primitive symbols.[3] Classical approaches thus may be said to represent knowledge in a relatively low-density, coarse-granularity fashion. They are designed to represent fairly directly what has been called "structured information,"[4] that is, information that can be formalized as rules or at least as explicit propositions or statements. They are primarily symbolic rather than numerical in their computations, although they may employ probabilistic techniques to qualify the certainty or uncertainty of their results. Conceptually, their algorithms are serial, although parallel computational hardware may be employed to increase speed in particular implementations. Classical approaches model or mimic cognitive phenomena that occur in humans on time scales of one second or more. They employ deductive and inductive inferencing. They engage for the most part in monotonic inferencing.[5]

Connectionist approaches show a different set of commonalities. Connectionist systems are composed of massive numbers of densely interconnected units that act in parallel. "A single unit may correspond to a neuron, a cluster of neurons, or a conceptual entity related in a complex way to actual neurons."[6] Connectionist systems store information by altering the strengths of the connections between the units. Their knowledge representation may thus be said to be relatively high-density and fine-grained. Moreover, network behavior is an emergent property. Knowledge is not stored in particular units but is distributed throughout the network. "Learning" takes place via algorithms that use numerical information available locally at the unit level; local changes in connection strengths give rise to learning at the network level. Connectionist systems are designed to represent "unstructured information," that is, information that has not been or cannot be formalized. The systems learn from examples (so-called supervised learning) or from experience (unsupervised learning), rather than from explicit statements or rules.[7] They are capable of generalizing their knowledge to new situations. They exhibit graceful degradation of performance when units fail or when input data are noisy. They match or classify patterns holistically rather than relying on deductive or inductive reasoning. Conceptually, their algorithms are parallel, although they are most often implemented through simulations on serial hardware. They model or mimic cognitive phenomena that occur in humans on time scales of less than one second.

An important but sometimes overlooked point about connectionist systems: Basically, a connectionist network constructs or estimates a multidimensional mathematical function that represents the network's target knowledge domain. The network may be said to be a very sophisticated curve-fitting program. A designer need not, and often cannot, specify the form of the knowledge representation function in advance; rather, the designer specifies the network geometry and learning procedure, and the network itself constructs the function as it learns from examples or experience. The storage of data as a knowledge representation function contrasts with the pigeonhole- or mailbox-like memory of a classical AI system.

Connectionist systems' ability to generalize to new situations may be viewed as being a result of the mathematical properties of the knowledge representation function. The network constructs a function based on a training data set,[8] attempting to find the best fit to sampled data. The function so constructed runs smoothly between sample points. The network thus responds easily to new data falling between sample points. Of course, the representation of data as a smooth function also creates the potential of confusion or cross talk. The function is an abstraction of the training set, and a network may fail to construct a function sufficiently complex to permit the distinction of every sample from every other sample. Such confusion is reminiscent of the memory confusion human beings sometimes exhibit.

Hoopla, Hype, and Hacks

Workers in artificial intelligence, unlike most scientists, almost never acknowledge their difficulties and are highly sensitive to criticism.
—Hubert Dreyfus and Stuart Dreyfus, *Mind over Machine* (1986)

Various AI researchers, both classical and connectionist, have from time to time overstated the performance of their computer programs, especially as regards the ability of these programs to produce intelligence comparable to human intelligence. Such overstatement may or may not be typical of most AI workers and probably is heard less frequently today than in years past. Some of the researchers' hype may have been deliberate, made during sales pitches to customers or grant agencies. Nonetheless, the popular press has sometimes believed the hype. And unfortunately, the researchers have sometimes believed it, too.

A little debunking may be in order. It is not true that AI systems are intelligent in the sense that humans are, or that AI researchers are at this time anywhere close to building a computer as intelligent, say, as HAL in the movie *2001: A Space Odyssey*. It is not true that the classical AI programs known as "expert systems" can truly replace human experts, or that they reason the way human experts do. Expert systems can occasionally outperform human experts and can be valuable aides to human experts, but they cannot do the sort of sophisticated, contextual, situated judgment that human experts do, usually automatically.[9] Likewise, it is not true that the popular reference to connectionist systems as "artificial neural networks" means that connectionist systems are miniature brains. Nor is it true that the "neurons" that compose the computational elements of connectionist systems are anything more than highly abstracted representations of biological neurons, or that the "learning" of connectionist systems is anything more than a highly abstracted version of the learning that takes place in biological neural systems.

The term "artificial intelligence" itself is potentially misleading. The term is used at least three different ways. It is used to characterize computer science research related to the ultimate goal of creating a machine intelligence, that is, a computer program or system that exhibits intelligence comparable to human or animal intelligence. It is also used to characterize computer programs that attempt to model certain aspects of human intelligence so that such processes may be better understood in their own right. Finally, it is used to characterize computer programs that automate certain tasks that traditionally could be performed only by humans. These computer programs may operate according to principles having little to do with the way human cognition operates. Often, the programs' designers have no pretensions about modeling human intelligence; they simply want to get the task done. Possibly, confusion among these different uses of "artificial intelligence" may have in some measure contributed to some AI researchers' apparent self-delusions that their particular research projects were accurate models of human intelligence. More likely, the converse is true. (Despite the ambiguity, the term "AI" will be used in all of these senses, and perhaps others of which I am unaware, throughout this essay.)

Another reason for AI hype is the so-called first-step fallacy.[10] When a research direction achieves an impressive success early on, people may tend to believe, falsely, that its success will continue. Certainly this was the case with classical AI, and critics argue that it is also the case with connectionist AI. In both cases, after first flushes of enthusiasm, difficulties have arisen, and at least in the case of classical AI, those difficulties appear to be fundamental.

It may be worthwhile at this point to review some of the limitations of both classical and connectionist approaches. The short version of the criticism levied against classical approaches is that they require a lot of ad hoc tweaks ("hacks," in computer jargon) in order to be made to do anything worthwhile. Although not entirely fair, this observation contains a large grain of truth. Classical rule-based expert systems, for example, may contain rules that employ ad hoc threshold or cutoff values used to discriminate between categories of input. As another example, there seems to be no general theory of how to design the frame data structures in classical frame-based systems. More generally, classical approaches tend to be brittle, prone to catastrophic failure, and do not respond well to new situations. They are seldom capable of learning from examples or from experience. They may be difficult to program in those cases where it is difficult to get human experts to articulate their expertise in the form of rules, which turns out to be very often. Indeed, it seems that human experts seldom use rules, and that step-by-step, rule-by-rule procedures are more characteristic of novice practice than expert practice. Experts employ sophisticated patterns of situational responses, patterns that for them have become nearly automatic. When asked, they must go out of their way to articulate how they do what they do.[11]

In some respects, classical approaches' limitations are connectionist approaches' strengths. Connectionist systems have successfully performed certain pattern-recognition tasks such as converting printed English words to intelligible audible speech, tasks that humans do seemingly effortlessly and that classical AI approaches traditionally have done only with great difficulty and limited ability. Connectionist systems can display bidirectional associative memory. For instance, a LEXIS-like connectionist system designed to associate case names and keywords not only can recall the cases associated with a given keyword but can recall the relevant keywords if given the name of a case. Connectionist systems exhibit graceful degradation and learning and require no articulation of rules.

But connectionist approaches also require hacks. In a connectionist system, there are numerous design parameters that are chosen more or less ad hoc, including the number of units (nodes) in each layer of the network and the number of layers; the number of connections between nodes; the geometry of those connections; the initial distribution of connection weights prior to training of the network; the choice to use nodes that represent abstract neurons or nodes that represent more complex data (microfeatures), and if the latter, which microfeatures should be encoded; the coding of the input and output data; the selection and presentation order of training data; and the learning algorithm and its rate coefficients. The designer may be unable to predict in advance how long the network will need to be trained, whether it will achieve an optimal solution to a given problem, and how well it will generalize to new situations not present in the training data.[12]

Unlike classical systems, connectionist systems cannot describe the chain of inferences used to achieve a result, simply because they do not operate via sequential inferencing. And, as noted earlier, connectionist systems, unlike classical systems, may confuse their stored memories.

Critics argue that a crucial first-step fallacy in connectionist systems is the so-called scaling problem. As researchers move from relatively small networks, containing perhaps tens of units and hundreds of connections and operating on toy problems, to relatively large networks, containing thousands of units and hundreds of thousands or millions of connections and operating on real-world data, the networks take progressively longer to train. Other difficulties may arise as well. Dire predictions that connectionist systems will soon be swamped by the scaling problem have so far failed to come true; connectionist researchers admit that the problem is real, but many are taking a wait-and-see approach to dealing with it. Some hope that parallel hardware implementations may help mitigate the scaling problem. It should be noted that some recent theoretical work on scaling in connectionist systems admits that theoretical predictions about the scaling problem may have some limitations of their own. This theory concerns a supervised learning system's ability to load *all* its performable tasks using a given learning algorithm. But the relevant practical question may be the network's ability to load a useful subset of those tasks. Likewise, the theory is concerned with *guaranteeing* 100 percent of the time that a given network will learn to do a task correctly 67 percent of the time. But the relevant practical question may be a more probabilistic measure of the network's ability to learn.[13]

Classical and connectionist AI approaches have been subject to some common criticisms. The approaches share some common limitations. Both classical and connectionist systems operate on highly restricted, narrow knowledge domains. No good general theory exists of which tasks they will perform well, and which they will fail to perform. Some argue that because of the need for hacks, neither classical or connectionist approaches lead to a coherent theory of machine or human intelligence, or even to a reliable design methodology for task automation systems. Conversely, some argue that without a theory of human intelligence, AI of any kind must ultimately rely on hacks.[14] Both sets of approaches are faulted for assuming that knowledge can be cordoned off into independent domains that can be learned by a machine that has no larger context of general knowledge. And as will be discussed in the next subsection, both sets of approaches are faulted, rightly or wrongly, for a lack of biological realism.

The limitations of classical AI approaches have become apparent especially in the past few years. The limitations of the early versions of connectionism were brought to light in the late 1960s; the limitations of current versions are less clear, and of future versions, of course, yet unknown. It was a long time before it became widely believed that classical AI researchers were hitting fundamental limits. It is to be hoped, although not necessarily expected, that as the early flush of enthusiasm for connectionism winds down, connectionists will admit their limitations more readily than have classical AI workers. In all cases, critics should remember to differentiate among the three different types of AI: creating machine intelligence, modeling human intelligence, and automating tasks.

Criticisms of AI are sometimes born of a healthy skepticism. Awareness of limits and skepticism about results is particularly warranted in light of AI's history of overstated claims. However, the criticisms are sometimes born of infighting. Vocal minorities in both the classical and connectionist camps have championed their particular approaches with an almost religious fervor while denouncing competing approaches as being at best misguided and at worst totally wrong.[15] Thus it is important to critique the critiques. It is more helpful to think of AI not as a quest for the holy grail or philosopher's stone of machine intelligence but as a toolkit, a collection of approaches that may be useful for different purposes in different circumstances. The various aspects of intelligence that are reflected in greater or lesser degree in different AI approaches should not be mistaken for the whole of intelligence.[16]

Biological Realism

Both classical and connectionist approaches have been faulted for a lack of biological realism. AI systems, it is said, do not represent accurately the problems humans do or the processes humans use to do them. Classical approaches for the most part assume either that human cognition proceeds through formal or verbal mechanisms, or that the mechanisms of human cognition are irrelevant. Connectionist approaches, although seemingly biologically motivated, are criticized as being too far removed from biological reality to tell anything interesting about human beings. These criticisms have some truth, but only some.

Classical AI has rightly been criticized insofar as it claims to attempt to produce machine intelligence or to model all of human intelligence. At a very basic level, classical AI approaches assume that knowledge may adequately be represented by context-free or purely syntactic constructs, and that intelligent reasoning need not depend on embodiment in a human, animal, or robot body or on being situated in a social or cultural context.[17] But classical AI has achieved some very impressive results in the task automation area. Furthermore, it would seem that human beings, when viewed on time scales greater than one second, do at least sometimes engage in inductive and deductive reasoning. Humans certainly do a great deal more than this; nevertheless, classical AI was developed by reference to *something* that humans do. Classical AI, through its failures as much as its successes, may teach cognitive scientists a great deal about human reasoning in the long run.

Connectionist AI means different things to different people. To some critics, connectionism means the backpropagation technique, the most common form of connectionist system used in current research. These critics claim that backpropagation cannot reveal much, if anything, about human intelligence. Backpropagation is a supervised learning regime. That is, a backpropagation network cannot learn on its own but must be presented with input-output pairs, often tens of thousands of times, in order to be trained. Backpropagation networks have separate learning (training) and memory retrieval (performance) modes; unlike human beings, they cannot learn while doing. The networks are just three layers deep and have relatively few units and connections compared with biological systems. There are no feedback connections between input and output units in backpropagation networks. The networks do not operate continuously, as do biological brains, but rather in discrete stimulus-response cycles. Perhaps most important, say the critics, the units in backpropagation networks are at best extremely simplified, abstracted versions of biological neurons—so simplified that arguably they should not be likened to neurons at all.[18] A somewhat more expansive view of connectionism recognizes that backpropagation is not the only technique available. Unsupervised learning networks with feedback have been built, and these networks can simultaneously learn and remember. The critics point out, however, that these networks, too, rely on highly simplified neurons. The most expansive view sees connectionism as not being limited to currently available techniques, but rather as a philosophy—that the study of human and machine intelligence should attempt to take into account, and to explore, the properties of biological neural networks. On this view, the term "connectionism" would apply to techniques not yet developed as well as to those currently available. It would apply, for instance, to a system that consisted of multiple networks joined together in an architecture modeled after the complex structure of human or animal brains.

Proponents of connectionism believe that in spite of the simplifications currently employed, connectionist systems show important network-level properties such as the ability to learn from examples, the ability to generalize, and graceful degradation, properties that must be accounted for in any theory of intelligence. They stress that connectionist approaches have led to plausible mechanisms that could support these properties in biological neural systems. For example, connectionists point out that biological neurons are slow compared to electronic computers, with response cycles on the order of milliseconds rather than microseconds. It follows that if a biological neural network responds to a stimulus in a second or less, the algorithms employed by that network can have at most one hundred steps (100 steps times 10 milliseconds per step equals 1 second). Connectionist systems obey this hundred-step rule; classical systems do not.[19] It is still an open question what relationship the mechanisms used by connectionist networks bear to the mechanisms used by biological neural networks. The simplifications of connectionist networks may or may not obscure crucial properties of biological networks and may or may not overemphasize unimportant properties. Moreover, some connectionist research pays explicit attention to addressing the simplifications and taking first steps toward moving beyond them.[20] Proponents hope that the current generation of systems is the first in a series of approximations leading to an ever-increasing understanding of the nature of intelligence.

Critics who say that connectionist approaches are no more biological than classical ones overstate the case. Connectionist approaches make some attempt to emulate anatomical or neurobiological structures or computational processes; classical approaches do not. At most, classical approaches model certain logical or psychological processes of humans. But to say that classical approaches are totally irrelevant to what humans do is also to overstate the case. Ultimately, the question is, Under what circumstances is it appropriate to abstract away from biology in the ways that classical AI does? There may be something to be learned by so abstracting, at least in the first instance, so long as researchers do not mistake the abstraction for the underlying reality.

Both classical and connectionist approaches are faulted for assuming that intelligence can be achieved by a disembodied agent unsituated in a social and cultural milieu. Classical approaches usually do not incorporate mechanical or software-simulated robot sensory or motor capabilities, and when they do, such capabilities are seen as adjuncts to intelligence, mere input and output mechanisms, rather than as integral to intelligence. Classical AI approaches often have presupposed that intelligence could arise from purely syntactic manipulation of linguistic symbols. Connectionist approaches strive more than classical approaches for biological realism, and many applications of connectionism are in the nature of sensory or sensory-motor systems such as visual pattern recognition or pronunciation of printed words. Connectionist approaches may be more compatible than classical approaches with epistemologies that suppose that knowledge is constructed by intelligence rather than preexisting and discoverable by intelligence. Nonetheless, like classical AI systems, most connectionist systems *in the current generation of technology* mimic human brains and bodies only in a very limited fashion and have no concept of society or culture. Both classical and connectionist systems presently take an approach that may be likened to assuming that intelligence lies solely in the cerebrum and operates in isolation from the rest of the brain and nervous system and from the world. This approach corresponds to a picture of a brain-mind divorced from sight and sound and hands and hunger, a picture that does not square with recent thinking in philosophy, linguistics, and neurobiology. To dissect intelligence by working on one aspect of it at a time is a sensible research program, but one must be careful not to conflate the dissection with the intact organism.

As computer science continues to progress and, in particular, becomes more closely linked with other cognitive science disciplines, it seems plausible that at some point in the future, the most powerful computers may become more humanly intelligent, and indeed more like humans. Internally, computers may comprise heterogeneous specialized subunits that mimic anatomical or cognitive brain or mind structures. Externally, "the line between the computer and the robot is going to blur."[21] Human-like computers will also interact socially, with each other as well as with people. They will incorporate in their design an ever-better understanding of how human intelligence operates in a social and societal context, and of how evolutionary biology has shaped human nature and human society. These ideas seem consistent with the spirit of biological realism that characterizes connectionism at its best.

Bringing Together Classical and Connectionist Approaches

Classical and connectionist approaches represent attempts to solve different parts of the problem of intelligence. We come closer to solving the overall problem by using both sets of approaches together than by relying on either set alone.[22] Undoubtedly, computers in the future will have aspects that might be called classical, aspects that might be called connectionist, and many aspects that we have not yet seen.

One way to integrate classical and connectionist approaches in the same system is to make use of the fact that connectionist approaches deal primarily with phenomena on time scales of less than one second and classical approaches deal with phenomena on time scales of greater than one second. Thus in a hybrid system the different approaches may be used to handle computations on appropriate time scales in the context of a larger problem. When a human being engages in an extended chain of thought in order to solve a problem, the final answer is the last in a series of conscious impressions or thoughts. These impressions come in a series connected by associations that may or may not seem logical, and much of the thought process may be hidden from consciousness. Today, some connectionist systems process the inherently serial, greater-than-one-second time scale reasoning aspects of a computation by treating the connectionist network processing as a subroutine to be called iteratively by a conventional serial computer program. In an intelligent machine, perhaps intermediate results might be computed by multiple connectionist networks operating in parallel, and series of intermediate results might be chained together by classical inferencing. More likely, the connectionist and classical aspects of the machine could not be so neatly separated as this simplistic picture suggests.

A word should be said here about so-called *localist* systems. Like the *distributed* systems that have been equated with connectionist systems up to this point, localist systems comprise large numbers of densely interconnected units. However, localist systems differ from distributed systems in that each unit in a localist system is uniquely associated with a proposition or other linguistic or conceptual symbol similar to the sort of symbol normally found in classical AI programs. Nevertheless, localist systems do exhibit some emergent properties at the network level. Some AI researchers consider localist systems to be connectionist; others reserve the connectionist label for distributed systems. In this essay, the term "connectionist" generally refers to distributed systems; where localist systems are intended, they will be identified as such. It should be noted that the line between localist and distributed systems is not sharp. For instance, in some distributed systems the input or output units are associated with words, propositions, or other abstract symbols, and in some localist systems the connection strengths between units can be modified in response to learned stimulus patterns.

Classical AI systems may exhibit certain attributes typically associated with connectionist systems, and vice versa. Advanced classical systems may be capable of dealing gracefully with inexact fit through probabilistic confidence propagation, metarules, and other techniques and may be able to classify inputs along multiple dimensions. A hypothetical rule-based system having an enormous number of rules operating in parallel, with sufficiently dense cross-linking of rule inputs and outputs, might best be described in localist connectionist terms.[23] Connectionist systems may someday be built that exhibit classical sequential and symbolic processing capabilities.

Fuzzy Approaches

Recently, a third set of AI approaches has emerged. Fuzzy AI applies the mathematics of fuzzy sets and fuzzy logic to create what are being termed fuzzy expert systems. In the United States, the chief proponent of fuzzy AI is the University of Southern California's Bart Kosko. Fuzzy systems are in commercial use in Japan but have not yet been widely accepted in the United States. Indeed, the whole topic of fuzzy theory is considered somewhat controversial, and some proponents of classical expert systems are skeptical that fuzzy systems add anything to classical expert systems employing certain types of probabilistic techniques (confidence propagation).

Fuzzy theory is based on the notion of partial set membership. Whereas in classical logic, an item either belongs to a set or does not, in fuzzy logic, an item may have a fractional set membership. This is said to be distinguishable from classical probability methods, which may assign an a priori probability that an item is or is not in a set, but which assume that a posteriori, the item will prove to be either in the set or not. Kosko gives the example of an apple in the refrigerator: There is a 50 percent probability that you will find an apple in the refrigerator; but if you find half an apple in the refrigerator, the thing you just found is 50 percent in the set of apples and 50 percent not in the set of apples. In short, fuzzy systems deal not with what is probably true but with what is partially true.

Fuzzy AI may be seen as yet another bridge between classical and connectionist approaches, although it has unique aspects as well. Like a connectionist system, a fuzzy expert system acts as a function estimator for a function that is not explicitly specified ahead of time. However, the fuzzy system's function is fuzzy; it is not a mapping from a well-defined set of input points to a well-defined set of output points but from an input fuzzy set to an output fuzzy set. A reduction to an exact-valued function is usually performed as a final step in the computation. Also like a connectionist system, a fuzzy system employs algorithms that are conceptually parallel; however, the parallelism is of a low order, comparable to that in a parallel hardware implementation of a classical system. The fuzzy system may use iteration to process the inherently serial aspects of a computation, that is, to do the aspects of the computation that in humans occur on greater-than-one-second time scales. Like classical systems, fuzzy systems allow the designer to work with verbal or structured knowledge, specifying system design through verbal rules. However, the rules are fuzzy, specifying imprecisely their preconditions and conclusions, and easily permitting the simultaneous entertainment of contradictory hypotheses. A fuzzy rule might say something like, "If the velocity of the pendulum is pretty small, then increase the correction motor input a little"; the designer specifies the meanings of "pretty small" and "a little" according to (usually simple) mathematical formulas. Conceptually, in a fuzzy system, all rules fire, or rather *partially* fire, at once. This is as opposed to a classical system, in which a rule either does or does not fire when its preconditions are met. Fuzzy rules may be specified by a front-end connectionist system, thus integrating the fuzzy and connectionist approaches.

It remains to be seen whether fuzzy systems will prove to be an important addition to the AI toolkit. Kosko asserts that fuzzy systems and connectionist systems have important commonalities and considers them as aspects of a single discipline. Like classical and connectionist systems, fuzzy systems have their share of hacks, such as the choice of the mathematical functions used to represent fuzzy ranges of values in fuzzy rules and the choice and coding of the fuzzy rules themselves. Also, the problems of debriefing experts in order to convert expert knowledge into (fuzzy) rules, although less severe than for classical AI systems, are by no means eliminated. And the system's set of rules is fixed by the programmer and cannot be fundamentally changed by the system, which again is similar to the analogous limitation in classical AI systems, and to the limitation posed by the separation of learning and performance modes in many connectionist systems.[24] Finally, the system's fuzzy output must somehow be made determinate in practical applications. One must evaluate the significance of the hacks in the context of whether the goal is to create machine intelligence, model human intelligence, or accomplish a given task.

Fuzzy systems' prototypical applications are in real-time control systems, whereas connectionist systems' prototypical applications are in holistic pattern-matching problems, and classical systems' prototypical applications are in non-real-time diagnostic or reasoning problems. For example, a fuzzy system has been developed that solves the problem of backing a simulated truck up to a simulated loading dock. The same problem has been done with a connectionist system.[25] But a more prototypical problem for a connectionist system might be to recognize the loading dock from a distance, or to recognize a certain model truck in a photograph of a parking lot. Presumably, the backing-up problem could also be done with a suitable classical system (although perhaps with great difficulty and ungraceful degradation of performance); but a more prototypical problem for a classical system might be to figure out the order in which boxes should be stacked to pack the truck most efficiently, or to diagnose the nature of the truck's mechanical malfunction given a list of its symptoms.

Although classical, connectionist, and fuzzy AI approaches can be adapted to many situations, each has been developed most extensively for certain classes of problems. On a given problem, even where all three kinds of approaches provide solutions, one kind may allow a solution to be most easily perceived. At the same time, the others may provide important insights. Even if fuzzy logic ultimately proves to be analytically reducible to probability theory, it provides a new way of thinking about problems, and that is significant in its own right.

Legal AI Systems

Researchers have designed quite a number of AI systems for legal applications. Although most such systems are still experimental, a few are in real-world use at private law firms and in government, notably at the IRS. Some well-known examples of legal AI systems include L. Thorne McCarty's TAXMAN and Anne von der Lieth Gardner's contract offer and acceptance expert system. A fairly extensive literature on legal AI systems has developed. This section presents a taxonomy of legal AI systems, classifying them according to the type of task they perform, the area of substantive law with which they are concerned, the source of their legal information, and their role vis-à-vis human actors and placing them in the larger context of office automation. The section continues with a consideration of the contributions of classical, connectionist, and fuzzy approaches to legal AI systems, as well as what may be learned through the development of these systems, and concludes with a brief discussion of the practical impact of these systems.

Taxonomy

Legal AI systems serve primarily to automate or partially automate analysis tasks and planning tasks. An analysis task consists of applying the law to a given set of facts, possibly developing hypotheticals in the process. Analysis tasks are typical of oral and written argument in litigation. A planning task consists of developing a course of action designed to bring about a desired final state of affairs from a given initial state. Planning tasks are typical of corporate, tax, or fiduciary practice. They may be more challenging for AI systems than analysis tasks because they have relatively fewer constraints. Whereas in an analysis task the facts remain more or less fixed, the object of a planning task may be to achieve a fundamentally changed set of facts. Most legal AI research to date has focused on analysis tasks.[26]

Legal AI systems may also automate or partially automate data retrieval tasks, document-drafting tasks, and training tasks. These support tasks complement the analysis and planning tasks, and may be integrated with them. Data retrieval tasks involve "intelligent" search for case law or other documents. Document-drafting tasks involve generating documents automatically. Training tasks include computer-assisted instruction for practitioners and students and may someday include computer-assisted oral-argument practice for upcoming trials. All of these support tasks have already been implemented to some extent in conventional computer technology, but AI technology may lead to more powerful implementations. An AI-based data retrieval system might employ search strategies that reflect the structure of the substantive law; imagine, for example, an automated horn-book or treatise that can interpret a fact pattern sufficiently well to retrieve the relevant sections of the book, along with the cited cases and statutes. An AI-based document-drafting system would take the first steps of customizing a form contract or will, or might write the first draft of a legal argument. As AI is introduced into support-task automation, the distinction between support tasks and the principal analysis and planning tasks may begin to blur. For instance, a system that helps an attorney construct a legal argument may integrate factual and legal analysis, data retrieval, and document-drafting components. However, it should be emphasized that the examples just presented are still in the laboratory or in the future.[27]

Legal AI systems cover a number of areas of substantive law, including contract offer and acceptance, asbestos tort claims, trade-secret misappropriation, estate planning, employee discharge, worker's compensation, immigration and naturalization, and statutory negligence law. An extensive variety of applications has been developed in the area of tax law. Because AI systems work well only on narrow domains of information, the systems do not purport to cover entire bodies of law but restrict themselves to small subsets.

Legal AI systems draw principally from three sources of legal knowledge. The first and most important is the written law, including case law, statutory law, and secondary sources such as rules, official directives, handbooks, restatements, and legislative history. The second is practical know-how. This includes the hands-on expert knowledge of attorneys, paraprofessionals, or government officials: how to find the law, how to craft an argument, to whom one should turn with a particular problem, problem-solving strategies that have worked before, in-house documents and resources, unwritten procedures, and the like. Know-how also includes the implicit knowledge of the structure of the law encoded in legal indexing systems. The third source is legal theory, which is usually implicit in system design rather than represented explicitly.

Legal AI systems may be designed to aid attorneys, clients, secretaries, paraprofessionals, law students, judges, legislators, or government functionaries—in short, all legal actors.[28] Some systems are designed to interact directly with clients, automating routine work that would otherwise be done by an attorney or paraprofessional. Such systems may be especially useful in nonlitigation contexts. It has even been proposed that a system could be designed for use by two parties in an arm's-length bargaining relationship to allow them to begin to draft the terms of a contract without assistance from an attorney.[29]

For the most part, however, research has concentrated on systems tailored for use by attorneys. Hugh Gibbons has developed a theoretical framework identifying the various ways AI might be used to assist a practicing attorney. The framework specifies the eight phases of an attorney's workflow as fact gathering, factual analysis, legal analysis, normative analysis, strategic planning, tactical planning, plan implementation, and client feedback and indicates how AI might be employed at every phase. Gibbons proposes that analysis, planning, and support tasks be considered not in isolation but as integral parts of the overall workflow. He speculates that a lawyer's workstation may someday be designed that would integrate software tools for all phases in a way that would maximize the attorney's productivity while adapting transparently to her work style.

Legal AI systems are but a subset of the AI systems and other software systems that will shape the law office in years to come. The attorney who wishes to use legal AI tools to boost office productivity will need to consider such tools as part of a total package of software-based office automation. Legal AI software will need to be integrated with word processing, workflow management, accounting, interactive video, and other office software. Indeed, the software systems that most directly affect lawyers' day-to-day practice are likely to be the AI systems not targeted specifically at lawyers. At some point in the future, personal computers and workstations are expected to offer capabilities such as handwritten input and, possibly, voice input. Attorneys who need to convert handwritten notes from meetings or depositions into finished documents will be able to take advantage of the fact that their notes, written on electronic rather than paper notepads, can be downloaded directly into their word processors for editing. Attorneys who prefer dictation to typing may be able to dictate directly into their word processors. Handwriting-understanding and voice-understanding technologies have traditionally been considered to be AI technologies, but as they become commercially available, they may come to be regarded as conventional. Whatever they are called, these new technologies will redefine the work style of the attorney and the relationship between attorney and secretary.

Classical, Connectionist, and Fuzzy Approaches

Designers of legal AI systems may consider using classical, connectionist, or fuzzy approaches, alone or in combination. To date, virtually all legal AI systems have been classical, probably because the other approaches are still relatively new. Many of the classical systems have been rule-based expert systems. Perhaps this is because of the intuitive appeal of mapping rules of law into the formalism of these systems. It may also be because from a practical standpoint, legal AI systems succeed best where the substantive law is well-defined, which very often is to say, where the law may be expressed as explicit rules.

AI systems that simulate case-based reasoning have also been developed. For example, Kevin Ashley's HYPO system classifies trade-secret misappropriation cases by locating them within a multidimensional case description space. The dimensions of the space correspond to ways in which the various cases in HYPO's database are more or less like one another for purposes of adjudication. HYPO can construct hypotheticals for the attorney's consideration by varying the facts of a case along the relevant dimensions. HYPO's approach is somewhat reminiscent of connectionist approaches in that a connectionist network may be regarded as a means of classifying input patterns according to their location in a many-dimensional space. However, a connectionist network creates its own classification space, developing the appropriate classification dimensions as it learns from exemplars. In HYPO, by contrast, the classification dimensions are prespecified by the programmer.[30]

Perhaps the best example of connectionism (more precisely, localist connectionism) in a legal AI system is the SCALIR legal information retrieval system being developed at UC San Diego. SCALIR is a legal research tool, a cousin of LEXIS and WESTLAW, but it allows far more powerful searching than do the standard tools. SCALIR represents cases, statutes, and keywords as units in a hybrid classical-connectionist network. The network interconnections are of three types: classical links, which represent fixed logical interrelationships among cases or statutes, for instance, that one case overrules another or that one section of a statute cross-references another; hybrid links, which represent logical interrelationships subject to revision or dispute, for instance, that one case limits or criticizes another; and connectionist links, which are the heart of the system and which represent the strength of associations among various elements in the network, for example, between different cases and between cases and keywords. The attorney using SCALIR not only can use keywords to suggest cases but can run the system bidirectionally, using cases to suggest keywords, which in turn can suggest other cases, and so on. SCALIR retrieves entire networks of related cases, statutes, and keywords simultaneously and visually displays a network so retrieved via a powerful graphic interface. The attorney can move through the network at the click of a mouse. SCALIR is designed to learn from experience, forming new associations in its network in response to patterns of attorney usage. For instance, SCALIR can learn to associate a relevant case with a keyword even when the keyword does not actually appear in the case. It can also learn to ignore or to de-emphasize cases so well known to the attorney that displaying them would be a waste of time. In general, the more SCALIR is used by a group of attorneys, the more it comes to reflect their legal know-how.[31]

An example of a distributed connectionist legal AI system is Lothar Philipps's simple backpropagation network designed to compute damages in two-person automobile accident cases decided under German law. The network consists of a set of input units that stand for the truth of propositions about the cases, such as whether the first party failed to signal; a layer of hidden units; and a single output unit whose value varies from -1 to $+1$ according to the distribution of damages between the parties. The network learns from sample cases and extrapolates to new situations. It has been tested on problems with small numbers of input propositions.

No published research has yet developed a working fuzzy legal expert system, although there have been attempts to apply the mathematics of fuzzy sets and fuzzy logic to law. Some authors have argued that fuzzy logic can be of no use in legal AI, but their critiques predate Kosko and appear not to fully appreciate the potential conceptual leverage provided by the fuzzy approach. As was mentioned earlier, even if a fuzzy system can be shown to be mathematically identical to a suitably designed classical system, the two are not identical from the standpoint of the designer's vision, and one or the other may prove more effective from the practical standpoint of getting a working system up and running.

Lessons and Insights

Writing any computer program, and especially an expert system, forces one to be extraordinarily rigorous and precise in one's thinking about the underlying subject matter and almost inevitably adds to one's understanding of that subject matter, often in ways unforeseen at the start of the project. Research and development of legal AI systems can provide new insights about legal reasoning, substantive law, and practical lawyering.[32]

One of the goals of AI is to model human performance. Legal expert systems, like most classical AI systems, use highly simplified models of human reasoning, and the limitations of these models can be highly instructive. McCarty's TAXMAN made it clear, for instance, that legal concepts are not fixed but are constructed and modified during the course of a difficult case.[33] In general, as will be discussed more fully later in this essay, classical AI systems may be seen providing a telling demonstration that formalist models fail to capture the nature of human reasoning.

With regard to substantive law, the experience of organizing a body of law into a form readily accessible to a computer may illuminate previously hidden aspects of the law's structure. Areas of law where "further definition may be appropriate or necessary" become clear. Structural regularities may become apparent when previously separate multiple-indexing systems or other information sources are incorporated in one AI system. Legal AI systems may provide a convenient mechanism for testing intersections of proposed and current laws.[34]

Gardner states that AI systems in law practice are no substitute for human judgment. Gibbons, in showing the ways AI might be integrated into an attorney's workflow, stresses that at every step, the attorney must make sophisticated human judgments. These judgments cannot and should not be automated. So long as expert systems use rules and human experts do not, and so long as AI's goal of machine intelligence remains unrealized, the importance of human judgment cannot be overstated. A legal AI system designed to work directly with clients is at times best off giving the following advice: "Call an attorney."[35]

Philosophy and AI

The advent of AI has had important implications for philosophy. The questions raised correspond roughly to the first two goals of AI. Attempts to create machine intelligence have raised the question of whether machine intelligence can ever be attained. Attempts to model human intelligence have led to new ideas about the nature of human intelligence.

Intelligent Machines

Philosophers and computer scientists continue to debate, often fervently, whether a truly intelligent computer can ever be built. It is of course not yet known what attributes give rise to intelligence or to consciousness. Suggestions include the incorporation of certain kinds of feedback loops in information processing, a certain rate (bandwidth) of information processing, the presence of language ability, or the development of a concept of self. Some theories stress the importance of innate goals or drives. Perhaps consciousness is a process rather than a state or a thing. Intelligence may require that a machine have a body. Some would say it requires a soul as well.

A related problem is whether we would know an intelligent machine if we met one. The standard Turing test for intelligence places the observer in one room, another human in a second room, and the possibly intelligent machine in a third room. The second human and the machine communicate via teletype with the observer. The observer poses questions to the other two, and if she cannot tell which responses come from a machine and which from a human, the machine is considered to be intelligent. But it is not clear that a truly alien intelligence would pass the Turing test. For instance, dolphins are sometimes thought to be as intelligent as humans, yet it is not clear how to perform a Turing test with one, if only because we cannot yet speak any dolphin language with sufficient fluency and because even if we could, the dolphin's experience would be so different from our own that, assuming interspecies communication about complex issues were possible, the dolphin's answers might turn out to be dead giveaways. Moreover, a very intelligent creature might fail to pass the Turing test simply because it found the game too uninteresting to be worth playing.[36]

It is also unknown whether a machine that exhibited intelligent behavior would necessarily have the subjective experience of consciousness. Perhaps an intelligent machine's sight, for instance, would be like the blindsight sometimes observed in neurologically damaged patients. A blindsighted patient cannot "see" a light held in front of her yet can "guess" with accuracy far better than random chance the direction from which the light is coming. Nor is it clear to what degree an intelligent machine need be conscious, or how frequently. A human being's dreams are products of her intelligence but not of her waking consciousness. A sleeping human being cannot pass the Turing test until she awakens. The myriad states of consciousness that characterize human experience—sleeping, waking, daydreaming; trance, hallucinatory, and ecstatic states; and so many others—may or may not prove to be integral to intelligence.

Many resist the idea of intelligent machines. Even theorists whose approaches seem compatible with an information-processing view of intelligence may go out of their way to dissociate themselves from such a view.[37] The machine-intelligence debate often takes an impassioned tone. Skepticism born of AI's history of hype seems to combine with a fear that proponents of machine intelligence may turn out to be right. Perhaps underlying the debate is a fear that machines may be used to replace people, or to control people, or to judge people. On this view, machine intelligence, even if possible, ought not to be allowed. Those who believe in and favor machine intelligence may respond that intelligent machines may be humanity's best hope for long-term survival. No definitive answer is yet possible. Intelligent machines are still science fiction.

The Mind-Machine Metaphor

Computer models of human intelligence are premised on the metaphor of mind as machine. In this metaphor, thought is seen as information processing, and the brain is likened to a very powerful computer whose workings are not yet well understood. Arguably, the mind-machine metaphor is actually a pair of metaphors: The mind is seen as machine, and certain machines are seen as minds.

The mind-machine metaphor is used to understand both artificial and human intelligence. Human logical inferencing is seen as the rule-by-rule working of a classical expert system. The technical literature speaks of "case-based reasoning" and "rule-based reasoning" performed by legal AI systems, even though computers cannot "reason" in the human sense of the word. Connectionist systems are viewed metaphorically as brains or other biological neural networks. Learning, generalization, and confusion behaviors exhibited by connectionist systems are seen as similar to human behaviors called by the same names. The brain and the computer are seen as different species of information-processing machines. Biological neurons become "wetware." A mind is understood to be an information-processing machine of sufficient and properly structured complexity, whether carbon- or silicon-based. Interdisciplinary cognitive science, in which philosophy, psychology, linguistics, neurobiology, and computer science merge in a larger academic discipline whose goal is the understanding of the workings of the mind, is possible because all of the component disciplines share a conceptual metaphor of mind as machine.

Like any metaphor, the mind-machine metaphor is a way of understanding one domain of knowledge in terms of another. The central question of AI is sometimes posed as, *Is the mind a machine?* but a better formulation is, *In what respects is the mind a machine, and what sort of machine is it?*

Perhaps not surprisingly, as computer science has developed, the sort of machine that philosophers and cognitive scientists understand the mind to be has changed as well, not so much because of computer science's progress as in parallel with it. In philosophy, the image of brain as digital computer is the basis for Hilary Putnam's influential doctrine of functionalism. In his recent rejection of functionalism, Putnam claims he no longer wants to view the brain as a computer. But a more accurate statement may be that he no longer wants to view the brain as a classical AI system, or as any disembodied, unsituated AI system. Connectionism, broadly construed, may in fact fit Putnam's new philosophy. In linguistics, George Lakoff has moved from disembodied, purely syntactic notions of language to a theory in which embodiment and metaphor play central roles. Lakoff gives a scathing critique of standard analytic philosophy in general, and of classical AI in particular, but suggests that connectionism, done right, is not subject to the same criticism.[38] In psychology, connectionism has likewise been influential.[39] Fuzzy AI has apparently not yet had an impact similar to connectionism's impact, but that may change in time.

The human mind is able to go beyond black and white and deal in shades of gray, to think holistically as well as sequentially, to deal in categories that have blurry boundaries and seemingly odd interconnections, to entertain multiple, contradictory competing hypotheses, and to accept reasoning that does not lead to determinate conclusions. Fundamentally, the human mind is not a classical AI machine, and theories that suppose that it is are bound to be limited in ways analogous to the limitations of classical AI.

A Thought Experiment

> *Put in your earplugs*
> *Put on your eyeshades . . .*
> — The Who, "We're Not Gonna Take It,"
> from the rock opera *Tommy* (1969)[40]

Strip away sense data, layer by layer. Imagine yourself without sight. Imagine yourself without hearing, without touch, without smell or taste. Imagine no sense of bodily position or movement, no feelings of hunger or thirst or internal sensation. Strip away memory as well. Imagine yourself without future or past, without a concept of time, without past images or feelings to ground the present. Now strip away language. Strip away beliefs, desires, and goals. At what point in peeling away these layers do *you* as a distinct being disappear?

In some sense, we are no more than the sum of our psychic parts—or, more properly, an emergent property of these parts. Yet we maintain the subjective impression that there are independent *I*'s inside our heads somewhere, entities that experience sense and memory rather than being constructed of sense and memory. The impression becomes less solid from time to time and may deliberately be dissolved, as in some Eastern spiritual disciplines, but it is part and parcel of our everyday waking lives.[41]

The *Gedanken* just described turns once more on the mind-machine metaphor, in some sense. The notion that the mind is simply the emergent property of an organized set of mental functions (in connectionist terminology, a parallel distributed computation) presupposes that the mind may be discussed in functional terms, and specifically in functional information-processing terms. This is not to say that other metaphors for mind might not also lead to a similar result, only that the *Gedanken* coheres with the picture of the mind developed on the mind-machine metaphor.

The point of the thought experiment is to emphasize the embodied and contingent nature of mind. The Cartesian skeptical position is possible only up to a point. The act of skeptical doubt presupposes doubting not only sight and sound but internal bodily sensation; if all sensory data are doubted, and all past sensory data are likewise doubted, the *I* begins to vanish. *I think, therefore I am* presupposes abstraction, connected logical thought, and self-awareness, which in turn presupposes memory. Without memory, one thought could not connect to the next; the *I* in the first clause would not connect with the *I* in the second clause. The very words *I think, therefore I am* presuppose language; language is part of what constructs the *I* in the first place. The disembodied mind-machine is no mind at all.

Interactionism

Rodney Brooks builds robots. As the head of the Mobile Robots (Mobots) project at MIT's Artificial Intelligence Laboratory, Brooks leads an effort to build robots inspired more by insect intelligence than by traditional notions of human intelligence. Crucial to this effort is the idea that intelligence is in the world, not in the head: "It is soon apparent, when 'reasoning' is stripped away as the prime component of a robot's intellect, that the dynamics of the interaction of the robot and its environment are primary determinants of the structure of its intelligence."[42] Brooks's work exemplifies a set of AI approaches that may be termed interactionist AI, or simply, interactionism.[43]

Creatures

The Mobots project, begun in 1985, has built a number of robots. Some examples are Herbert, Genghis, Squirt, and Tom and Jerry. Herbert is a large robot that wanders around the laboratory seeking empty soda cans, which it steals from people's desks and brings back to a bin at its starting location. Genghis is a small six-legged robot that walks somewhat in the manner of a crawling insect, successfully negotiating rough terrain. Squirt is a tiny wheeled vehicle that hides in dark corners and moves when it hears noise. Tom and Jerry are toy cars that, among other things, chase people. Other robots have been or are being built as well, such as Toto, which explores its way around the laboratory and remembers landmarks, thus enabling it better to find its way in the future.

Brooks's robots share a common design philosophy. The robots "are Creatures in the sense that . . . they exist in the world and interact with it, pursuing multiple goals."[44] They operate in the real world; specifically, they move freely through the offices, corridors, and laboratories of the MIT AI Lab, and they deal successfully with collision avoidance and other contingencies of the real-world environment, including people who may deliberately try to confuse them. They do all this with minimal central control and no explicit symbolic computation. The robots generally do not maintain internal models of the world; instead they use the world as its own best model and respond to changing conditions in the world as the conditions arise. Such models as they do maintain are decentralized, activity-oriented representations that are constructed in real time by the robots themselves rather than ahead of time by humans. Brooks's robots perform their seemingly intelligent actions with minimal amounts of computation; some, such as Tom and Jerry, do not even employ microprocessors.

To implement this design philosophy, Brooks has developed a software architecture called the subsumption architecture. Multiple layers of control implement relatively simple behaviors; higher-level behaviors can either incorporate or override lower-level behaviors. The behaviors combine to produce the robot's overall performance. Levels are more or less autonomous, so that a Brooks robot has no central locus of control, no single place in the computational system that "knows" what the robot is doing. Rather than communicating through a central computer, the layers of behavior interact with each other through the medium of the world itself.[45]

At the lowest level, for example, a robot might have a collision-avoidance behavior. A robot executing this behavior will sit in the middle of the room until its proximity sensors detect something coming too close, at which point it will move away, avoiding collisions as it goes. After a certain time, it will stop and wait again. At the next level up, the robot might have a behavior that causes it to wander about randomly. With both behaviors active, the robot will wander but will still avoid collisions.[46] At a still higher level, the robot might have a behavior that attempts to get close to warm objects such as people. When no one is nearby, the robot will wander and avoid collisions as before; but when a person comes near, the robot will suppress its wandering behavior and close in on the person. However, the collision-avoidance behavior will keep it from actually hitting the person. Another higher-level behavior might be to attempt to get close to walls. If the robot sees a wall, it will head toward it; however, the collision-avoidance behavior will keep it from actually hitting the wall. If the robot is headed at an angle to the wall, the combined wall-reaching and collision-avoidance behaviors cause the robot to follow the length of the wall. Still more complex behaviors, such as Herbert's soda-can grabbing and Genghis's complicated six-legged gait, emerge through similar kinds of interactions of simple behaviors.[47]

Another example emphasizes that lower-level behaviors need not be especially reliable in order to give rise to sophisticated and reliable higher-level behaviors. A robot has been developed that follows moving objects, such as radio-controlled toy trucks or notebooks dragged by strings, across the floor. The robot accomplishes this in part by means of a vision system that incorporates two simple, unreliable routines. The first routine detects motion in the robot's visual field; the second routine attempts to pick out the image of an object in the vicinity of the motion detected by the first routine, and to track the subsequent motion of the object thus found. The robot attempts to move in such a way as to keep the object's image centered in the visual field. The object-tracker routine often loses the object, and the motion detector routine is noisy, but usually one routine succeeds where the other fails, and together, the two routines permit the robot reliably to follow moving objects, even in poor-contrast conditions.[48]

Brooks takes his philosophy of distributed control beyond the level of the individual robot. Brooks has suggested that with the advent of micro-machines—microscopic electric motors and other mechanical parts crafted on silicon chips in much the same manner now commonly employed to make electronic circuits—entire robots could be built on single chips. This would allow tasks traditionally performed by single large machines (either robot- or human-driven) to be performed instead by hordes of gnat-sized, expendable robots. Brooks proposes, for example, that gnat robots designed to eat dirt in carpets be used to replace vacuum cleaners, or that miniature explorer robots replace the single large rovers traditionally used for lunar or planetary exploration.

Brooks self-consciously avoids trying to model human intelligence. He states that AI researchers should learn from the experience of nature. In nature, insect intelligence preceded human intelligence; moreover, nature took far longer to evolve from amoebas to insects than from insects to humans, which may suggest that the hard part of the problem of intelligence is the insect part.[49] Therefore, insects are a good place to begin. Many of Brooks's robots look and act in a manner reminiscent of insects, and even the human-sized Herbert may best be thought of as an overgrown insect robot. Nevertheless, the subsumption architecture can provide a noncentralized, nonunitary model of intelligence that may equally well be applied to humans and to insects. In this respect, it complements some recent theoretical literature in AI and in neuroscience suggesting that the human mind may better be viewed as a collection of semiautonomous, unintelligent or semi-intelligent processes operating in parallel, with little or no central control.

Humble Phenomena

Philip Agre received his Ph.D. from the MIT AI Lab in 1988. His dissertation, "The Dynamic Structure of Everyday Life," incorporates both computer science and philosophy and calls for a rethinking of AI grounded in an appreciation of "the mind-blowing intricacy of humble phenomena."[50] Like Brooks, Agre rejects approaches to AI that place intelligence in the head rather than in the world, and Agre regards Brooks's work as the AI research program closest to his own.[51] Unlike Brooks, however, Agre is principally concerned with human intelligence.

Agre's dissertation describes, among other things, Pengi, a robot (actually, a computer simulation of a robot) designed to play the video game Pengo. The protagonist in Pengo is a penguin who lives in a world populated by ice cubes and killer bees. The bees try to sting the penguin or pelt it with ice cubes; the penguin tries to avoid the bees and to hit them with ice cubes. Apparently, Pengi plays a pretty good game of Pengo. Although not built with the subsumption architecture per se, Pengi nonetheless shares certain important characteristics with Brooks's robots. In particular, Pengi embodies the minimalist computational approach that characterizes Brooks's work. Like Brooks's Tom and Jerry, its logic is so simple that it can be implemented without a microprocessor.[52] Also, Pengi does not attempt to plan ahead and then execute its plans. Instead, like Brooks's robots, it improvises to fit the situation at hand. Although some of Pengi's behaviors may be seen as goal-directed, its action is the result of a continual interplay between its perceived world and its simple internal logic. Similarly, rather than maintaining abstract or objective representations of the objects in its video world, Pengi represents these objects with respect to the penguin's activity. Whereas a classical AI Pengo-playing program might have representations for things like ICE-CUBE–41, Pengi has representations for things like *the-ice-cube-I-am-now-kicking.*

Agre's dissertation also describes, in remarkable detail, episodes from Agre's everyday life intended to show the complex patterns of human interaction with the world. Agre describes, for example, his daily trip from his apartment to the subway. He notices minutiae such as how he has learned almost unconsciously to avoid being hit by a certain low-clearance tree and how he navigates through a parking lot whose cars are never in the same arrangement from day to day. Agre seeks to find repeated or underlying patterns of world interaction that characterize human activity. He sees episode studies as indicative of the kind of work that AI needs to do in order to understand and emulate human intelligence.[53]

One of Agre's main themes is that human activity is a process of continual improvisation, of "continually redeciding what to do."[54] For instance, a person opening the door to an apartment need not be concerned with the exact orientation of the keychain buried in a coat pocket. The person simply fumbles around from moment to moment until a grip is achieved and almost unconsciously reorients the keys to fit the lock in the process of withdrawing them from the pocket. Likewise, a person given simple instructions on how to get from Agre's apartment to the subway stop can negotiate the way without being told to maneuver around a particular fence, avoid a certain pothole, or watch for traffic. Moreover, the person who is told to cross Essex Street will succeed in doing so even though there is no street sign indicating that the street in question is in fact Essex Street.

Agre's episode studies suggest that many complex human behaviors emerge as the product of numerous lower-level behaviors interacting through the medium of the world—in much the same manner as occurs with Brooks's robots. His descriptions are particularly interesting because they involve verbalizations of low-level behaviors that most people take for granted most of the time. According to Agre, it is precisely those human activities that seem so trivial as to be not worth discussing that are essential to intelligent behavior. And it is because these activities are seldom noticed and difficult to verbalize that AI tends to de-emphasize or devalue them.

Comparison with Classical, Connectionist, and Fuzzy Approaches

> *It is unfair to claim that an elephant has no intelligence worth studying just because it does not play chess.*
>
> —Rodney Brooks, "Elephants Don't Play Chess" (1990)

Interactionism contrasts most sharply with classical AI. Unlike classical AI, interactionism espouses minimal computation and minimal central control, eschews symbolic computation and abstract internal models of the world, and avoids making plans as distinct from executing them and improvising on them. Whereas classical AI traditionally supposes that the important problems of intelligence are those involving language and abstract reasoning, and that the problems of perception and motor skills can safely be assumed away, interactionism suggests that perception and action are hard problems and, moreover, that "simplifying" the constraints of the world makes reasoning harder, not easier.

On the interactionist view, the real world is not a hostile place from whose dangers a robot or other AI system must be shielded, nor is it a noisy environment from which meaningful data can, with difficulty, be extracted through sophisticated processing techniques. Rather, the real world is a benign or even benevolent place. For the most part, real-world biological organisms spend their time going about regular routines, and dilemmas or problems are the exception rather than the rule. When problems are encountered, they are usually solved in the context of ongoing activity, rather than in isolation. Whereas abstract problems tempt the programmer to seek perfectly general solutions, the constraints of the real world serve to limit the range of solutions to problems. Likewise, in the real world, organisms do not solve problems from scratch each time but learn from experience and even modify their environment to make their problems easier. Interactionist AI imports these observations about real-world biological organisms into the context of real-world robots. The world is the robot's partner. It works, or even dances, with the robot as the robot works or dances its way through the world.

Like connectionism, interactionism seeks a certain amount of biological realism. Like connectionist systems, interactionist systems are constructed of distributed computational elements based on very simple hardware. Often, the computational elements are so simple that they can scarcely be called computers. Unlike connectionist systems, however, interactionist systems have only minimal internal wiring connecting their computational elements. Rather, the computational elements interact through the medium of the environment. Nor do interactionist systems attempt to model or pattern themselves after neuroanatomy. Like connectionist systems, interactionist systems attempt to take into account the computational constraints posed by the fact that biological creatures need to react in real time to changes in their environment. In connectionist systems, this is done by way of the hundred-step rule; in interactionist systems, it is done directly by requiring that the systems perform in real time in real-world environments. Both connectionist and interactionist systems rely on emergent properties thought to have analogs in biological creatures. In connectionist systems, complex network properties emerge from interconnected simple component units; in interactionist systems, complex behaviors emerge from interacting simple component behaviors.[55]

Like fuzzy AI systems, interactionist AI systems work in real time and are designed to deal with an inexact and imprecise world. Unlike fuzzy systems, however, interactionist systems do not maintain systemwide time clocks or attempt to categorize the world, even inexactly, in terms of abstract internal models. One can imagine an interactionist version of the fuzzy truck backing-up system described earlier. A truck Mobot could presumably be designed to back up to a loading dock in response to some external stimulus. Just as Herbert's can-grabbing behavior subsumes behaviors such as collision avoidance, locating soda cans, and positioning Herbert's hand properly with respect to the can so that the can may be picked up, the truck's backing-up behavior would subsume lower-level behaviors such as collision avoidance, locating the loading dock, and aligning the truck's body perpendicular to the dock. Unlike the analogous fuzzy system, however, the interactionist system would maintain no explicit internal representation of the truck's position or angle with respect to the loading dock.

Interactionist AI has more or less the same goals as other kinds of AI: creating machine intelligence, modeling the performance of humans or other creatures, and automating tasks. However, these goals are reinterpreted somewhat because interactionism does not view intelligence as something that exists in the abstract, and it is concerned with ongoing dynamic behavior rather than with discrete tasks. In interactionism, task automation is accomplished as a by-product of intelligent interaction with the environment.

The danger of the first-step fallacy applies to interactionism as much as it does elsewhere in AI. Although Brooks, in particular, has scored some great successes at the outset, it is too early to tell whether his approach will after some time prove to be relatively limited and much more difficult to extend than was first envisioned. It is not yet known how complex a behavior can be accomplished with limited internal world representation and no central control.[56] Moreover, although Herbert and other Mobots may be able to learn landmarks or sensor calibrations, the Mobots as yet cannot learn brand-new behaviors and can reorganize the interactions between their component behaviors only to a limited extent. Again, it remains to be seen whether the robot technology can be extended to afford such learning and reorganization. Finally, it is unknown how far the interactionist approach can go, especially with regard to developing machine intelligence, without taking into account in detailed fashion the biology, particularly the neuroanatomy, biomechanics, and social behavior, of living creatures. To date, although the behaviors exhibited by interactionist systems may in some instances resemble in greater or lesser degree the behaviors of natural biological creatures, the means by which such behaviors are accomplished may have little to do with the means employed by natural creatures. The choice of behaviors incorporated in interactionist robots remains more or less ad hoc. In principle, an intelligent robot of the future need not operate according to the principles of biologically based intelligences. Nevertheless, biological systems are still the only known systems that exhibit demonstrable intelligence. To the extent that these systems can successfully be understood, they may serve to provide valuable insights and models for AI. Machine intelligence may be easier to achieve if biological intelligence is used as a blueprint. Then again, attempts to design intelligent machines from the ground up may lead to new understandings of biological intelligence.

Rethinking the Mind-Machine Metaphor

There is a traditional notion that human intelligence resides solely in a detached, unitary, more-or-less centralized entity or system called the mind. Thought, not activity, is considered primary. Thinking is viewed as a matter of solving discrete problems rather than coping with ongoing processes. Perception, cognition, and action are conceptually distinct. In AI, this notion of intelligence is most closely associated with classical approaches.

Interactionism adopts a very different view of intelligence, one in which intelligence is seen as arising from the dynamic interaction between an organism (not necessarily a human being) and its environment. On this view, intelligence is not something that creatures have, but a description of what they and their environments interactively do. Interactionism calls into question the notion that creature and environment need to be seen as entities that are conceptually separate from one another and conceptually separate from their processes or activities. It abandons the idea that the mind is the source or locus of intelligence.

Interactionism shows that the organizing metaphor of AI need not be the usual mind-machine metaphor. In interactionism, the brain is not seen as a computer, at least not in the sense that computers are conventionally understood. Conventionally, computers are seen as problem-solving machines that receive information as input and produce other information as output. But in interactionism, dynamic interaction with the world replaces information processing as the primary concern. Interactionism sharpens the embodied, situated view of intelligence and takes it beyond the picture of an embodied, situated mind-machine by not only refusing to draw a sharp line between mind and world but also rejecting the notion that the brain, or even the organism, is the seat of intelligence. If anything, the brain-body-environment system is the machine, and intelligence, a description of the system in action.

Although interactionism redefines intelligence, it does not eliminate the question of what behavior should properly be called intelligent. How would we tell whether an AI system built on interactionist principles were sentient? The Turing test, based as it is on the inputs and outputs to and from a disembodied black-box mind, does not fit the interactionist picture of intelligence. To test an interactionist system for human-like intelligence, then, perhaps we would instead have to situate the system in a series of environments—a grocery store, an office building, a park—and see whether its behavior in those environments were indistinguishable from a human being's.

Of course, one of the test environments could be the sealed room setup of the Turing test. This raises an important point: Although interactionism is in the first instance a distinct set of approaches to AI, in the end, it is a way of viewing all intelligent systems. More generally, each set of AI approaches— classical, connectionist, fuzzy, interactionist—provides the basis for a set of potentially powerful metaphors through which to understand intelligence, metaphors that may find applicability beyond the particular implementation technologies or types of situations with which their respective AI approaches are prototypically associated. Viewed in interactionist terms, Herbert has neither any plan for finding and retrieving soda cans nor any internal model of them; viewed in classical and connectionist terms, Herbert follows rules for searching for soda cans and for returning to home base, engages in pattern matching when detecting soda cans in a cluttered environment, and, as a whole, has or embodies a working model of soda cans even though that model cannot be located in any of Herbert's component behaviors. A sentient robot that employed connectionist networks might be viewed in interactionist terms; conversely, although perhaps to a lesser extent, a sentient robot that employed the subsumption architecture might be viewed in connectionist terms. A human being playing a chess game or riding a bicycle may be viewed in terms of any of the AI approaches. Some metaphors fit some systems or situations better than others; still, we can choose to apply alternate metaphors.

3

Simulated Vehicles in the Park

Parallels may be drawn between AI and law, and between AI and jurisprudence. In particular, classical AI shows strong parallels with formalist jurisprudential theories.[1] The discussion that follows, and for that matter much of the rest of this essay, are to be understood as having a "broadly speaking" qualifier attached. The qualifier applies because it is potentially misleading to speak of all classical (or connectionist or fuzzy or interactionist) AI approaches or all versions of formalist (or realist or critical or pragmatist) jurisprudence in one breath. For instance, Langdellianism, the legal process school, and law and economics are all in some sense formalist; so are rule-based expert systems and logic programming. To speak of them all at once is to ignore a wealth of important differences. But the comparison intended here is metaphorical, not exact. The idea is to play with the notion of seeing legal reasoning as AI information processing, legal theory as AI computer science, and ultimately, law as an AI system.

The mind-machine metaphor, central to AI, appears in jurisprudence as well. Sometimes it is explicit, as in Jerome Frank's image of the judicial slot machine: Judging is seen as a process wherein cases are fed into the hopper of the machine, a crank is turned, and justice is dispensed at the output. Sometimes the metaphor is less obvious, as in the well-known image of the scales of justice, which implicitly represents the judicial mind as a mechanical balance. Sometimes it is quite hidden, for instance as a constitutive component of Holmes's marketplace-of-ideas metaphor. Even when the metaphor is not apparent, it may provide a helpful way of thinking about jurisprudential concerns such as how judges do and should make decisions, the nature of legal rules, and the relationship between law and society at large. And just as in philosophy and psychology, AI's new understandings of what sort of machine the mind may be may provide new ideas in jurisprudence. "Mechanical jurisprudence" need not have negative connotations if the "machine" becomes more human.[2]

Indeterminacy and Open Texture

Formalism and rule-scepticism are the Scylla and Charybdis of juristic theory; they are great exaggerations, salutary where they correct each other, and the truth lies between them.

— H. L. A. Hart, *The Concept of Law* (1961)

Truth and reference are intimately connected with epistemic notions; the open texture of the notion of an object, the open texture of the notion of reference, the open texture of the notion of meaning, and the open texture of reason itself are all interconnected.

— Hilary Putnam, *Representation and Reality* (1988)

Classical AI and formalist jurisprudence tend to place a premium on verbal, propositional reasoning, and to presuppose that such reasoning may be made arbitrarily precise. However, human reasoning is far more than propositional reasoning, and language is inherently indeterminate. Perhaps the appearance of formalist approaches in both AI and jurisprudence reflects prevailing philosophical or scientific undercurrents. But whatever the reason for their appearance, formalist approaches cannot, except in limited circumstances, cope with the complexity of human language.

Some of the issues common to AI and law arise in H. L. A. Hart and Lon Fuller's classic debate over a mythical ordinance that prohibits vehicles in the public park. The problem is what counts as a vehicle for purposes of the ordinance. A car qualifies, except that a police car sent to handle a crime presumably does not. A motorcycle is a vehicle for purposes of the ordinance; a perambulator is not; a bicycle, probably not; a moped, not clear. Fuller poses a law professor's hypothetical: May the veterans' local arrange to have an army vehicle mounted on a pedestal and placed in the park as a statue? And so on.[3]

The same problem can arise in AI. Consider a hypothetical "smart" automobile designed to navigate down ordinary streets and highways in response to English instructions. The automobile is told, "Proceed ahead one mile, and then make a left at the first light." The machine dutifully proceeds one mile and then continues to the next intersection thereafter, at which point it encounters four street lights; a traffic signal consisting of a red light, an amber light, and a green light; a flashing red light atop a stopped police car; and a neon sign at the corner diner. The bewildered machine now faces the problem of what counts as a light for purposes of its instructions—a problem analogous to the statutory interpretation problem posed by Hart and Fuller.

Language is indeterminate. Formal languages, it turns out, are radically indeterminate, as Putnam demonstrates. The indeterminacy of human language appears to be constrained by the human experience. Nevertheless, the process of interpreting human language in context is a process of inexact matching, if it is a process of matching at all.

A Partial Catalog of Indeterminacies

For purposes of this essay, a number of different indeterminacies may be distinguished. One sort of indeterminacy arises when the meaning of words or statements is clear as applied to some prototype or base case but becomes progressively less clear in cases progressively more different from the prototype. This sort of indeterminacy is observed in the vehicle-in-the-park problem. It is part of, or perhaps may be seen as the basis of, the general set of problems sometimes called open texture. Open-textured concepts are those "whose application to fact situations cannot be automatic" but must rather be "context dependent."[4] "Must" is the key word here. It might be thought from the vehicle-in-the-park and the streetlight examples that the problems of open texture are readily resolved by the expedients of sufficiently precise definitions and rigorous logic. This is not so. No deterministic procedure can be given for specifying the prototype or for mapping from the prototype to the difficult case. Open texture is fundamental and pervasive and inheres in the nature of thought and language.[5]

Open texture is one of a cluster of concepts that includes Wittgenstein's family resemblance, Hart's core and penumbra of meaning, Kuhn's paradigms (in the sense of exemplars), and Lakoff's radial categories. McCarty and Sridharan's prototype-deformation and Gardner's easy-hard case schemas represent attempts to incorporate open-texture indeterminacy into the structure of legal AI systems. Open texture occurs at the levels of words, phrases, statements, cases, concepts, theories, worldviews. "Word or concept" and similar phrases are often used in what follows to imply all levels of open texture.

Another sort of indeterminacy arises from changes in meaning over time. The language evolves, so that the prototype or "plain meaning" of a word or concept may evolve as well. Society changes, whether slowly or rapidly, so that existing words or concepts must be interpreted in novel situations, as when a court or agency must apply existing law in situations clearly unanticipated by the legislature, or when an AI system is called on to perform in a situation that could not even have been anticipated at the time of its design. Finally, the individuals who serve as authoritative interpreters of meaning are replaced, as when a swing-vote vacancy on the Supreme Court is filled. New people make new meaning.[6]

A third sort of indeterminacy is deliberate. A common law trial court does not attempt to define the law for cases other than the one before it. An appellate court may attempt to clarify doctrine by stating as clear a rule as possible, but it is understood that some indeterminacy remains to be worked out in future cases. Similarly, a legislature sometimes leaves to courts or administrative agencies the job of expounding key terms of a statute. The legislature may, for instance, wish to preserve established doctrine without having to specify it. Legislators may realize their own lack of prescience or may need to make political compromises to get a bill passed. Whatever the reasons, a statute may have intent and meaning that are at best not wholly clear. This is even more true for a constitutional provision.[7]

Legislative compromise suggests a fourth sort of indeterminacy, that of conflicting meanings or interpretations. Conflict may inhere in a single word or rule, as when lines of precedent diverge. At a higher level, conflict may arise when policies conflict or rules collide, as in the tension between the free exercise and establishment clauses of the First Amendment.[8] Fundamental to the adversary system is that plausible factual and legal arguments can and must be made on both sides, which presupposes indeterminacy of conflict at one or more word-concept levels.

One last sort of indeterminacy may be termed *essential vagueness*. The open texture of the vehicle-in-the-park ordinance could to some degree be mitigated by further definition. But some concepts are such that their indeterminacy cannot be reined in except in application to specific cases, and then often only in conjunction with other vague concepts.[9] Generally speaking, the more broad the concept, the more essential its vagueness. Due process, equal protection, and free speech are sweeping concepts that have given rise to two centuries of jurisprudence and scholarly debate; all would fall under this notion. The maxims of equity are likewise essentially vague.

Essential vagueness may be seen alternatively as another aspect of open texture. The core meaning of an abstract concept is far less clear than that of a simple concrete object, say, a chair. If one is asked to bring a chair into the room, one will not go too far wrong by bringing an upright four-legged chair with a backrest and seat, but one may go wrong if one brings, say, a beanbag chair. The core instance of chair is clear, whether because the human mind treats simple physical objects as conceptually basic, or because chairs are learned about early in childhood, or perhaps because chairs are designed to fit the human body and so must be more or less similar to one another.[10] Arguably, an abstraction such as due process also has a core meaning, perhaps that of a fair trial. But that core is itself an abstraction, or at least is more complex than the core instance of a chair. People are much less likely to agree on the essentials of the core of due process. Even if they do agree, there are many more ways to diverge from a complex prototype than from a simple one.

That language is indeterminate and open-textured does not mean that attempts to make legal language more precise ought to be abandoned. What it does mean, though, is that situated human judgment is required when interpreting even the clearest rule. At the same time, it also means that the fluidity of language need not trouble us.

Dancing

I'd like to meet you
In a timeless
Placeless place
Somewhere out of context
And beyond all consequences . . .
—Suzanne Vega, "Language,"
from the album *Solitude Standing* (1987)[11]

Consider two contrasting metaphorical descriptions of communication through language.[12] In the first description, language communication is seen as a process in which a sender, the speaker or author, transmits speech-objects or messages through an imaginary conduit or telephone line to a recipient, the listener or reader. The speech-objects are words or concepts, typically statements, that refer to the world and that wholly contain the ideas to be transmitted. In general, although the conduit is bidirectional, so that either party may be sender or receiver, a given message passes in one direction only. This fairly conventional picture of language communication suggests an orderly and exact process, mostly free from uncertainty. However, it hides several important aspects of language use. In real life, the speaker and listener participate in an ongoing mutual interaction, both verbal and nonverbal, with each other and with their world. Other speakers and listeners may be involved, directly or indirectly, in the conversation. The speaker and listener, together with their conversation and the language through which they communicate, participate in and contribute to a matrix or network of contexts ranging from their immediate local situation to the larger sociocultural milieu. Variations occur among individuals, groups, cultures, traditions. The speaker and listener may share some background assumptions and not others and may be partially or totally unaware of the ways their assumptions and contexts do not overlap. Seemingly clear language takes on differing significances for different participants in a conversation. In short, the conduit metaphor abstracts away much of the human world in which language communication takes place.

In the second metaphorical description, language communication is envisioned as a dance. The participants are partners. Their dance is an ongoing, dynamic interplay that combines stylized forms with improvisation. The dance requires not only the dancers but music and a room with a dance floor of some sort; these "background" or "contextual" ingredients of music and space are essential if there is to be a dance at all.[13] The partners are not detached subjects but are situated and engaged in the activity of the dance. Their dance may interact with or even combine with the dances of others who may be on the dance floor. This picture highlights the possibilities for uncertainty. The dance partners may be more or less acquainted with each other's steps or styles and may be more or less familiar with the music or with the particular room in which their dance takes place. The partners may hear the rhythm of the music differently from one another, and the music itself may change, either between dances or within a single dance. Even the room may change as other dancers enter or leave, the lights are raised or dimmed, or new sections of the dance floor are opened.

From the perspective of the conduit metaphor, the uncertainties associated with the aspects of language that are hidden by the metaphor may be seen as being distinct from and in addition to the five indeterminacies discussed previously. Uncertainties of significance and context are primarily associated with the speaker and listener and the background in which they converse; the various indeterminacies are primarily associated with the speech-objects themselves. For example, nominally factual statements that may or may not be especially open-textured, such as "I came here for the job opportunities" or "She had an abortion," may carry different normative significance for different individuals, depending on religious or political ideology, on moral or cultural values, or on social customs and manners.[14] As another example, a given statement may carry different significance depending on individual experience. The phrase "the feeling of the wind through your hair as you ride a bicycle down an open road" has different significance for one who has never ridden a bicycle than for one who has. A friend who studied abroad relates how the English phrase "the town square" for him conjures up images of a certain public square in his Midwestern hometown, and the equivalent phrase in Swedish conjures up images of a very different sort of public square, the one in the small Swedish town where he lived when he learned to speak Swedish. Differences in expertise give rise to differences in significance as well. "White's queen captures Black's pawn" may have a different significance to the novice chess player, who sees the move as advantageous, than to the grandmaster, who sees it as a misstep that will ultimately cost White the game. As a final example, in the core case in which an ordinary citizen purposefully drives an automobile into the park for no particular emergency and in deliberate disobedience of the ordinance prohibiting vehicles in the park, the rule clearly is violated, yet the rule's application may be uncertain. There may be no police around to observe the violation, or the rule may be selectively enforced by the police or the prosecutor.

From the perspective of the dance metaphor, distinctions between a statement's primary meaning and its secondary significance, or between indeterminacies of statements and uncertainties of background or context, do not make sense. The notion of language communication as an exchange of statements, and the correlative notion that statements may express their contained ideas more or less clearly, are simply absent from the picture. Uncertainty, rather than being associated primarily with the statements, the participants, or their contexts, is best viewed as associated with the communication-dance as a whole.

When the dance of language communication flows smoothly, uncertainty is incorporated seamlessly into its improvised structure. Thus the words "uncertainty" and "indeterminacy" seem somehow inappropriate to the dance metaphor because they connote the possibility and the hope that language may be made certain and determinate. Words like "spontaneity" or "inherent creativity" may fit better. Whereas "uncertainty" and "indeterminacy" suggest that the uncertainty of language is a problem to be overcome, "spontaneity" and "inherent creativity" suggest that it is a source of interest and inspiration. In law, the uncertainty of language may create possibilities for constructive legal change as laws and legal rules are reinterpreted in new times and situations.[15]

The conduit metaphor is consistent with formalist approaches in AI and jurisprudence. The metaphor underlies much of this essay's discussion; for instance, the essay speaks of the indeterminacies of legal rules as being associated primarily with the rules themselves rather than with the overall communication between law and society. The dance metaphor has an interactionist flavor and may be kept in mind as a helpful counterpoint to formalist views of language.

Stylized Examples

The simplification inherent in a formal model is also the source of its power and utility: it will often lead us to insights that would otherwise be obscured. . . . The unexpected consequences of our formulations may reveal surprising truths or, just as often, the inadequacy of the formulations themselves.

—L. Thorne McCarty, "Reflections on TAXMAN:
An Experiment in Artificial Intelligence and Legal Reasoning" (1977)

We can make the discussion of the limits of formalism somewhat more concrete by working through a simple example using a hypothetical classical AI system. The system is designed to apply logical inference rules to facts. The programmer begins by giving the system a set of rules and a set of facts. The system scans the rules and attempts to apply them to the facts in order to deduce new facts. As these new facts are deduced, the system adds them to its knowledge store. Once the system reaches the end of the set of rules, it begins scanning from the top again, attempting to deduce still more new facts. It continues scanning the rules repeatedly until it reaches some specified termination condition.[16]

In this system, a *rule* consists of an IF clause and a THEN clause. The system checks whether all the premises in an IF clause are true, and if they are, it adds to its store of knowledge a new fact representing the truth of the logical consequence of the premises. Such a rule is written in this form:

RULE # rule-number

IF (statement A_1 is true
    and statement A_2 is true
    and . . .
    and statement A_n is true)

THEN (record in system memory that statement B is true).

/* This space is used for the programmer's explanations and comments. */

Alternatively, in some rules, the THEN clause may specify an action to be taken by the system:

RULE # rule-number

IF (statement A_1 is true
    and statement A_2 is true
    and . . .
    and statement A_n is true)

THEN (take specified action).

/* This space is used for the programmer's explanations and comments. */

For either form of rule, the system assigns a unique arbitrary *rule-number* to each rule for record-keeping and cross-referencing purposes.

The facts of the system are stored in clusters called *frames*. A frame describes a real-world object as a list of ordered pairs of properties and values. Each property is called a *slot*. The frame's structure is analogous to a fill-in-the-blank form or template; each slot is a blank. The frame's *class* tells the general kind of real-world object the frame is supposed to represent. The system can easily group together different individual frames of the same class so that they may be processed in the same way. The system tracks interrelationships between frames of different classes by means of the *relatives* slot. For instance, a template for a frame of class CAR may be defined as follows:

```
FRAME # frame-number
    CLASS> CAR
    RELATIVES>
    MODEL>
    YEAR>
    COLOR>
    LICENSE>
    WEIGHT>
    BODY>
    TRUNK>
    OWNER>
    LENGTH>
    WIDTH>
    LOCATION>
    SPECIAL-FEATURES>
    NICKNAME>
```
/* This space is used for the programmer's explanations and comments. */

A template for a frame of class PARK may be defined as follows:

```
FRAME # frame-number
    CLASS> PARK
    RELATIVES>
    BOUNDARY-POINTS>
    NAME>
    HOURS>
    SPORTS-FACILITIES>
    WOODED-AREAS>
    SWIMMING-POOL>
    SPECIAL-FEATURES>
```
/* This space is used for the programmer's explanations and comments. */

Similarly, templates for other frame classes may be defined. The system assigns a unique arbitrary *frame-number* to each frame, again for record-keeping and cross-referencing purposes.

Given the template for a frame class, individual members of that class, called *frame instances*, are generated by copying the template and filling in its slots. The contents of any slot is called its *slot value*. A slot value may be a number, a word-symbol, a list of numbers or word-symbols, or another frame (represented by its frame number). Not every slot value need be filled in. A blank slot indicates that the value has not yet been determined; a slot value of "(none)" indicates that the slot specifically does not apply to the frame instance in question. Using the previous template for CAR, a frame instance for my Honda may look something like this:

```
FRAME # Q000
   CLASS> CAR
   RELATIVES>
   MODEL> Honda Civic
   YEAR> 1986
   COLOR> gray
   LICENSE> California 2EHW981
   WEIGHT> 1900 lbs.
   BODY> two-door hatchback
   TRUNK> (none)
   OWNER> Silverman, Alex
   LENGTH> 15 feet
   WIDTH> 6 feet
   LOCATION> (100, 300)
   SPECIAL-FEATURES> (none)
   NICKNAME> Old Paint
```

/* The CAR's LOCATION is assumed in this example to be specified in (X, Y) coordinates on an arbitrary grid. The BODY is specified here by a brief description but could instead be specified by a frame number. */

Rules and frames work together. The programmer starts the system off with a set of rules and an initial set of frames representing known facts. The system may add new frames to represent new facts it deduces and also may fill in or modify existing frames' slot values. The system runs down its set of rules repeatedly, adding and modifying frames until a rule representing a termination condition succeeds, at which point the system halts.

Simulating the Vehicle in the Park

The hypothetical AI system may be used to implement the vehicle-in-the-park problem.[17] A simple implementation includes frame definitions for

CAR, TRUCK, VEHICLE, PARK, and TICKET, plus four rules. One rule specifies what sort of real-world objects are VEHICLES. Another rule states that if any VEHICLES are found in any PARKS, an ordinance violation occurs and a TICKET should issue. A third states that if a TICKET is issued, the system should print it and halt processing. A fourth rule periodically asks the programmer whether any real-world objects have changed position, whether any new real-world objects ought to be added to the system, or whether the programmer would like the system to halt processing.

It is useful to consider each rule individually. The first rule, the one that checks for VEHICLES, considers every frame in the system. For each CAR or TRUCK frame found, it creates a corresponding VEHICLE frame. The CAR or TRUCK stores the frame number of the VEHICLE on its RELATIVES slot; this prevents the system from creating yet another VEHICLE frame for the same CAR or TRUCK every subsequent time it encounters the rule:

RULE # Q001

    IF (C is a frame of CLASS> CAR or CLASS> TRUCK
      and C has no RELATIVES)

    THEN (create frame V of CLASS> VEHICLE
      having RELATIVES> C
      and modify frame C's RELATIVES slot
      so that C now has RELATIVES> V).

/* C and V are variables, placeholders for frames or slot values. (Any other variable names could have been used.) The rule finds any CAR or TRUCK frame that does not yet have a corresponding VEHICLE frame, creates that VEHICLE frame, and causes the CAR or TRUCK and the VEHICLE frames to refer to one another. The rule ignores any CAR or TRUCK that has already been identified as a VEHICLE. It also ignores anything other than a CAR or TRUCK, such as a PARK, a STATUE, or another VEHICLE.[18] */

The second rule adds a frame of class TICKET to the system whenever a VEHICLE is found in a PARK:

RULE # Q002

    IF (V is a frame of CLASS> VEHICLE
      and V has RELATIVES> C
      and C is a frame of CLASS> CAR or CLASS> TRUCK
      and C's LOCATION is (X, Y)
      and C's LENGTH is L
      and C's WIDTH is W
      and P is a frame of CLASS> PARK

and P's BOUNDARY-POINTS are ((PX1, PY1), (PX2, PY2), . . . (PXn, PYn))

and LIES-WITHIN ((X, Y), L, W, ((PX1, PY1), (PX2, PY2), . . . (PXn, PYn))) is true)

THEN (create frame T of CLASS> TICKET
    having RELATIVES> (V, P)
    and modify frame V's RELATIVES slot
    so that V now has RELATIVES> (T, C)).

/* C, V, P, T, L, W, X, Y, and the PXs and PYs are variables. The rule finds a VEHICLE frame and looks up the corresponding CAR or TRUCK frame, which contains the information the system needs. The CAR or TRUCK is approximated as a rectangle of length L and width W centered at the location (X, Y). Next, the rule finds a PARK. The PARK is bounded by a polygon whose vertices are listed. Finally, the rule invokes the LIES-WITHIN function, not shown here, which the programmer must write and make available to the system. LIES-WITHIN geometrically compares the rectangle to the PARK's boundaries and determines whether a sufficient percentage of the rectangle's area lies within the PARK to count as being in the PARK for purposes of the ordinance. If so, the rule creates a frame of class TICKET and adds it to the system. The TICKET indicates, through its RELATIVES slot, which VEHICLE it affects and in what PARK the VEHICLE was found. The VEHICLE's RELATIVES slot now indicates both the CAR or TRUCK and the TICKET.[19] */

If the second rule succeeds, the termination condition of the third rule obtains, causing the system to print the ticket and halt processing:

RULE # Q003

IF (T is a frame of CLASS> TICKET
    and T has RELATIVES> (V, P)
    and V has RELATIVES> (T, C)
    and C is a frame of CLASS> CAR or CLASS> TRUCK
    and C's MODEL is M
    and C's YEAR is R
    and C's LICENSE is L
    and C's OWNER is O
    and C's LOCATION is (X, Y)
    and P's NAME is N)

THEN (PRINT-THE-TICKET using the information (M, R, L, O, (X, Y), N)
    and STOP).

/* C, V, P, T, M, R, L, O, X, Y, and N are variables. The rule finds any TICKET frame, looks up the VEHICLE and PARK to which it corresponds, looks up the CAR or TRUCK to which the VEHICLE corresponds, and uses the information on the PARK frame and the CAR or TRUCK frame to print the ticket. PRINT-THE-TICKET is a separate function, not shown, which must be supplied by the programmer. STOP is a standard function in most computer systems. In principle, this rule could be combined with the previous one. */

The final rule prompts the programmer for input:

RULE # Q004

IF (ALARM-CLOCK)

THEN (print on programmer's console, "Would you like to enter any new cars or trucks, or to halt the program?"
and run PROGRAMMER-INTERFACE).

/* Almost all computer systems provide a time-of-day function. Some also provide an alarm clock function; if not, the programmer must write one. The rule checks to see if the alarm clock has gone off. If so, the system prompts the programmer to update the information available to the system. The PRO-GRAMMER-INTERFACE subprogram, not shown, gives the programmer the opportunity to halt the system and to add, modify, or remove frames. The programmer must supply this subprogram. In a more sophisticated system, this rule might be replaced by one that updates information automatically. */

To summarize: The system is provided with the four rules, along with frame templates for CARS, TRUCKS, PARKS, VEHICLES, TICKETS, and possibly for other objects such as STATUES. It is provided with several frame instances of CARS, TRUCKS, and PARKS. It is also given instructions on how to perform various auxiliary functions such as LIES-WITHIN and PRINT-THE-TICKET. The system begins by deducing that the CARS and TRUCKS are VEHICLES. It then determines whether any VEHICLES are in any PARKS. If so, it prints out a ticket for each VEHICLE so found and stops. Otherwise, it continues scanning its rules indefinitely, occasionally prompting the programmer for input, at which time the programmer may halt the system or may update the system's information.

Problems with the Rule-and-Frame Implementation

The foregoing implementation of the vehicle-in-the-park problem cannot cope successfully with Fuller's hypothetical about the statue, for the system has no way to distinguish between a statue and an ordinary vehicle. To deal with this limitation, the programmer must find a way to represent the distinction between vehicles and statues in the language of rules and frames. The programmer's first instinct may be to define a frame class STATUE and then to rewrite the first rule, the one that tests for VEHICLES, as follows:

RULE # Q001A

   IF (C is a frame of CLASS> CAR or CLASS> TRUCK
      and C has no RELATIVES
      and C is not a STATUE)

   THEN (create frame V of CLASS> VEHICLE
      having RELATIVES> C
      and modify frame C's RELATIVES slot
      so that C now has RELATIVES> V).

   /* Based on old rule # Q001, with modifications as shown *in italics.* */

But because a frame in this system can be of one class only, *any* frame that is a CAR or TRUCK is not a STATUE. Moreover, the rule thus rewritten seems ad hoc. A more satisfying approach is to alter the frame definitions in an attempt to represent whatever it is that makes a vehicle a vehicle. But this turns out not to be so easy. Perhaps a vehicle moves people from one place to another and a statue remains stationary; but then a car abandoned in the park is a statue. Perhaps a vehicle rests directly on the ground and a statue is elevated; but then a private helicopter hovering in the park is a statue. Perhaps a vehicle has no pedestal, whereas a statue does; but then if Fuller's war veterans want to mount their truck directly on the ground, the way it was during the war, their truck is not a statue. So adding slots to represent things like PREVIOUS-LOCATIONS or HEIGHT-OFF-THE-GROUND does not seem to offer a robust solution. A third approach is for the programmer to use the RELATIVES slot to link any CAR or TRUCK that happens to be a STATUE to a STATUE frame. For instance, Fuller's example may be represented as follows:

   FRAME # Q005
      CLASS> TRUCK
      RELATIVES> # Q005A
      MODEL> Jeep
      YEAR> 1944
      COLOR> army green
      LICENSE> (none)
      WEIGHT> 2300 lbs.
      BODY> two-door open top
      TRAILER> (none)
      OWNER> World War II Veterans' Local
      LENGTH> 18 feet
      WIDTH> 6 feet
      LOCATION> (100, 300)
      SPECIAL-FEATURES> (none)
      NICKNAME> Old Reliable

/* The frame number in the RELATIVES slot indicates the STATUE frame that follows. */

FRAME # Q005A
   CLASS> STATUE
   RELATIVES> # Q005
   NAME> World War II Veterans' Memorial
   ARTIST> (none)
   YEAR> 1986
   MATERIAL> steel
   PEDESTAL> granite
   INSCRIPTION> "Dedicated to those who gave their lives for freedom"
   OWNER> City of Fullerton, California
   WEIGHT> 10,000 lbs.
   LENGTH> 23 feet
   WIDTH> 10 feet
   HEIGHT> 15 feet
   LOCATION> (100, 300)

   /* The RELATIVES slot indicates the preceding TRUCK frame. */

To process Fuller's example, the system begins with the rule that tests for VEHICLES:

RULE # Q001

   IF (C is a frame of CLASS> CAR or CLASS> TRUCK
      and C has no RELATIVES)

   THEN (create frame V of CLASS> VEHICLE
      having RELATIVES> C
      and modify frame C's RELATIVES slot
      so that C now has RELATIVES> V).

First the system tests whether the frame # Q005 is of class CAR or class TRUCK. Because the frame is a TRUCK, the test succeeds. Next, the system tests whether the frame has no relatives. The TRUCK does in fact have a relative, namely, the STATUE (frame # Q005A). Thus the TRUCK does not qualify as a VEHICLE and is not found to violate the ordinance.

Putting the STATUE on the RELATIVES slot, then, seems to solve Fuller's problem. The RELATIVES slot, whether it indicates a VEHICLE or a STATUE, seems to represent the manner in which human beings use the CAR or TRUCK. Unfortunately, the RELATIVES solution is still very much ad hoc. The programmer must specify in advance which CARS and TRUCKS are STATUES. All the system knows is that any CARS and TRUCKS that have predefined uses are not to be considered VEHICLES.

The system in no way understands how a vehicle is used, as the next example illustrates:

```
FRAME # Q006
    CLASS> CAR
    RELATIVES>
    MODEL> Matchbox toy Cadillac Fleetwood
    YEAR> 1990
    COLOR> aqua
    LICENSE> (none)
    WEIGHT> 3 oz.
    BODY> sedan
    TRUNK> 1 cubic centimeter
    OWNER> Chris, age 5
    LENGTH> 3 inches
    WIDTH> 1 inch
    LOCATION> (100, 300)
    SPECIAL-FEATURES> received as birthday present
    NICKNAME> "MY car!"
```

This CAR is not really a vehicle; in some ways, it is more like a statue. Of course, the programmer may again use the RELATIVES slot to show the use of the CAR by creating a new frame definition for frame class TOY, creating a TOY frame instance (say, # Q006A), and linking that TOY to the CAR in the same manner as the STATUE was linked to the TRUCK. But consider what happens if the programmer wants the system to exempt from the ordinance vehicles such as police cars, emergency vehicles, grounds-keeping and park maintenance vehicles, and the like:

```
FRAME # Q007
    CLASS> CAR
    RELATIVES>
    MODEL> Dodge police cruiser
    YEAR> 1990
    COLOR> black and white
    LICENSE> E789013
    WEIGHT> 3500 lbs.
    BODY> sedan
    TRUNK> 20 cubic feet
    OWNER> City of Fullerton P.D.
    LENGTH> 19 feet
    WIDTH> 6 feet
    LOCATION> (100, 300)
    SPECIAL-FEATURES> siren, flashing lights, two-way radio,
        on-board computer
    NICKNAME> (none)
```

Purely from a programming standpoint, there is no reason the police car cannot be treated analogously to the TOY and STATUE. The programmer simply needs to define a POLICE-CAR or EMERGENCY-VEHICLE frame class, creating a frame instance of that class (say, # Q007A), and link that frame to the CAR frame. But from a human standpoint, such treatment fails to capture the differences between the police car and the previous examples. Whereas the statue is a car that is no longer being used as a vehicle, and the toy is a car that can never be used as a vehicle, the police car certainly is a vehicle. It just happens to be a vehicle that does not violate the ordinance. To represent as much, the programmer must redesign the second rule, the one that tests whether a VEHICLE is in a PARK, to exempt certain VEHI-CLES, a job that is best left for another day.

Consider as a last example the following CAR, which is not a car at all:[20]

```
FRAME # Q008
    CLASS> CAR
    RELATIVES>
    MODEL> elephant
    YEAR> 1986
    COLOR> gray
    LICENSE> (none)
    WEIGHT> 4000 lbs.
    BODY> enormous
    TRUNK> 2.5 feet
    OWNER> Central Park Zoo
    LENGTH> 7 feet
    WIDTH> 3 feet
    LOCATION> (100, 300)
    SPECIAL-FEATURES> big ears, tusks, riders (mostly small children)
    NICKNAME> Baby Jumbo
```

As far as the system is concerned, this CAR qualifies as a VEHICLE in the PARK. Not only does the system fail to recognize that this CAR is an elephant, it also fails to recognize that it is a statue. The only consolation is that had it been a real elephant carrying riders through the park, the system quite properly would have asserted that it was being used as a vehicle and issued it a ticket accordingly.[21]

The Brittleness of Rule-and-Frame Formalism

"Socrates is mortal" is hardly more than a counter of logical text-books; S is M will do just as well—or better.

—John Dewey, *Experience and Nature* (1929)

The previous examples suggest that the rule-and-frame system fails to capture real-world meaning. The problems of the system are problems of knowledge representation—of how to organize, store, retrieve, and manipulate computer information in a manner that best addresses the task at hand. Knowledge representation is central to AI, and the type of knowledge representation used by an AI system characterizes it as classical, connectionist, fuzzy, or interactionist.

It is worth reemphasizing that the "knowledge" an AI system represents is not human knowledge. It is related to human knowledge only through the mind-machine metaphor. As the elephant example illustrates, the difference between a CAR and a car is more than one of capitalization. Frame classes and slot names are written in capital letters to emphasize that they are just empty labels, syntactic place markers devoid of content. For all the rule-and-frame system knows, the frame definition for CAR might just as well be

```
FRAME # frame-number
   CLASS> CAR
   RELATIVES>
   BXQZ>
   J48CQ1>
   XXXFAR>
   QWERTY>
   ETAOIN>
   . . . ,
```

with corresponding changes in the rules, such as

```
RULE # Q002

   IF (V is a frame of CLASS> VEHICLE
      and V has RELATIVES> C
      and C is a frame of CLASS> CAR or CLASS> TRUCK
      and C's XXXFAR is (X, Y)
      and C's J48CQ1 is L
      and C's ETAOIN is W
      and P is a frame of CLASS> PARK . . .
```

Ultimately, no matter what the programmer does, the rule-and-frame system does not have any sense of *why* a CAR is or is not a VEHICLE.

The simple foregoing vehicle-in-the-park implementation may overemphasize somewhat the ad hoc nature of rule-and-frame systems. Rule-and-frame systems of greater sophistication circumvent some of the problems of simple systems. For instance, frame systems may have built-in cross-check routines to ensure that slots take on only reasonable values.[22] Frames may be able transparently to take on the properties of frames of other classes via a mechanism called inheritance. Rule-and-frame definitions can be chosen carefully to anticipate and provide for the full range of cases with which the system must deal. However, cross-check routines and inheritance mechanisms are themselves somewhat ad hoc, and rule-and-frame definitions must be accompanied by suitable restrictions on problem domain. The problems of formalism in knowledge representation can be pushed back a level, so to speak, but cannot be eliminated.[23]

Rule-and-frame systems have trouble dealing with indeterminacy of all five sorts. The problems open texture poses for such systems are apparent from the previous examples. Likewise, changes in meaning over time, conflicting rules, and deliberate or essential vagueness do not fit a system that is based on deductive logic and that mandates precise definitions. Again, sophisticated systems may include features, such as the ability to deal with probabilities and the ability to assume facts as hypotheticals, that better equip them to deal with indeterminacy. Some frame systems permit slots to be added to existing frame instances, or even to all frames of a given class, without human intervention. However, such dynamic frame-structure modification greatly increases system complexity and can lead to hard-to-find programming bugs. Some systems have rules that can create other rules on the fly. But the rules so created are usually just minor variations on a template specified by the programmer. In the end, the programmer must anticipate the full range of system operation and must define directly or indirectly the allowable frame classes, slots, and rules.

The relationship between legal and AI rules is metaphorical. For people, perhaps 95 percent of cases are easy and 5 percent are hard; for an AI system, the converse is true at best. Legal rules are far more malleable and far less brittle than classical AI rules. Still, the experience of building a classical legal AI system can provide us with a unique sense or intuition about the limits of formalism and an enhanced appreciation of the role of human reason in law.[24] The vehicle-in-the-park system required a considerable amount of definition to achieve even the simplest results. An AI system based on a set of real-world legal rules, for example, a system such as an IRS tax expert system, requires far more. That such systems can be built suggests that formalism, despite its limitations, is powerful in suitably narrow contexts. At the same time, the literal-minded machine's need for so much definition makes apparent the role that common sense and contextual reasoning play in the interpretation of legal rules. It is human judgment that makes legal rules meaningful.

Categorization and Connectionism

Logic, a component of most legal arguments, fails to provide a natural framework for representing the overall processes of legal analysis and argumentation.
—Donald Berman and Carole Hafner, "Obstacles to the Development of the Logic-Based Models of Legal Reasoning" (1985)

Problems of categorization, decisionmaking, and judgment are central to both AI and law. An AI system, like a judge or legislator or attorney, must perceive the relevant facts in a situation, categorize or classify the situation according to rules or exemplars stored in its memory, make decisions, formulate plans, and take action. Both AI and law may create abstract models of the world, partly to ensure that judgments are made in systematic, logical, predictable fashion. The tension between the abstract models and the underlying reality drives both fields forward.

Categorization may be seen as a key element of all aspects of judgment. Facts are not prior to perception; people cognize facts through their categories of experience. Decisions, including those made more or less automatically, arguably represent categorizations of entire situations; an expert chooses to use a particular routine or procedure because it fits the category of the situation before her. If, as Dreyfus and Dreyfus suggest, expert-level cognitive processing constitutes more of what humans do, on a percentage-of-time basis, than rule-based or formal reasoning, then rule-based emulation of human decisionmaking will tend to fail, and to fail predictably. The indeterminacies of open texture, conflicting rules, essential vagueness, and so on that affect categorization of facts (substantive categorization) may be expected to affect categorization of situations (procedural categorization) as well.

Both AI computer science and American jurisprudential theory show tensions between formalist orthodoxies and more contextual or situated approaches. The brittleness of classical AI approaches arises in part from a failure to account for the core-penumbra structure of concepts, or the too-sharp demarcation of the core-penumbra boundary. In jurisprudence, Fuller speaks of the failure of correspondence theories of meaning; the limitations of classical AI approaches arise in part from a reliance on such theories. The graceful degradation of connectionist and fuzzy approaches reflects an ability to manage a smoother transition between core and penumbra. The emergence of connectionist and fuzzy approaches parallels and finds support in the emergence of postfunctionalist theories of meaning in philosophy.

Inexact Categorization

For the most part, classical AI systems categorize in yes-or-no binary fashion. The proliferation of slots on a frame or clauses in the IF portion of a rule reflects an approach to categorization based on making a multiplicity of bright-line distinctions. The notion that a frame belongs either to class X or to class Y, but not to both, likewise reflects binary thinking. To the extent that classical AI relies on propositional logic, on discrete rather than distributed knowledge representations, and on data representations that appear to be verbal formulations but that are in fact strings of purely syntactic place-marker symbols, classical AI is not well-suited for inexact categorization.[25]

In contrast, connectionist and fuzzy systems are designed from the ground up to be good at inexact categorization. These systems' abilities to match inexact input patterns and their graceful degradation of performance under conditions of noisy or corrupt data may be seen as machine analogs of the mind's abilities to deal successfully and transparently with open-texture indeterminacy. To the extent that in legal reasoning, there are usually two plausible answers to a question, namely plaintiff's and defendant's, rather than only one, connectionist and fuzzy systems may provide a closer analogy with legal reasoning than do classical systems.

Connectionist systems' ability to deal with indeterminacy may be seen as an emergent property of their distributed knowledge representations. Emergent properties are those that are exhibited by a system as a whole but that are neither localizable to any part of that system nor obviously similar to any local properties of system components. Douglas Hofstadter describes this phenomenon in his story of Aunt Hillary, the intelligent anthill. Even though each individual ant is dumb and knows only its local environment, the patterns of ants flowing in the hill have meaning. By analogy, the individual neurons in the brain, or simulated neurons in a computer, have no intelligence, but the overall pattern of their firing generates meaning. The meaning is not in the computational elements but in their connections. It arises synergistically from nonlinear interactions among the computational elements.[26] Thus, although the simulated neurons of a connectionist system operate according to mathematical formulas and are in that sense formalist, the system as a whole exhibits nonformalist properties. In contrast, classical systems do not exhibit nonformalist emergent properties. (If a classical system were to exhibit such properties, it would no longer properly be called classical.) The success or failure of a path of reasoning in a classical system can in general be traced back to a single point in the computation. Fuzzy systems, as might be expected, are somewhere in between, as their knowledge representations are less widely distributed than are those of connectionist systems.

Emergent properties are also seen in the human brain. Michael Arbib notes that the functional decomposition of the brain is not one-to-one with its structural decomposition.[27] More speculatively, emergent properties of the brain-mind may be seen as giving rise to cognitive phenomena including, ultimately, consciousness. Still more speculatively, open texture in language may be seen as an emergent property insofar as it occurs at the levels of words, phrases, statements, cases, concepts, theories, and world-views. The "speculatively" qualifier applies because the connectionist assumption that low-level neural networks scale up to explain high-level cognition, and the corresponding assumptions in brain and mind science, may yet turn out to be unfounded.

A Connectionist Vehicle in the Park

To illustrate the kind of thing that connectionist systems can do, consider a hypothetical connectionist associative memory designed to match words with corresponding pictured objects. Suppose the system were trained to recognize cars. Presented with a profile picture of a car, the system would output the name of the car; presented with the name, it would output the picture. For instance, presenting the system with HONDA would result in the display of a stored picture of a Honda. Presented with a blurred or partially obstructed picture of a car, the system would still output the name, albeit less reliably; the system might confuse the picture with that of another car. Presented with a picture of only the front half of a car, the system might even be able to retrieve the rear half of the picture as well as the name. Presented with a character string similar to two known names, but not the same as either, the system would output something in between the two corresponding pictures; for instance, presented with HYONDA, the system might display something between a Honda and a Hyundai. Finally, if some of the artificial neurons in the system were damaged and had to be shut off, the system would still perform, albeit with less accuracy.

One can also imagine a connectionist system designed to handle the vehicle-in-the-park problem. The system would be trained to distinguish between two classes of photographs of objects in the park, namely, those that contain vehicles (as defined for purposes of the ordinance) and those that do not. The system would be limited to still photographs and thus might very well fail on Fuller's statue problem. A system that would accept video rather than still photograph input would be more helpful; it could analyze the activity of a disputed object to see whether that object behaved as a vehicle. Unfortunately, it is not at all clear how to build such a system given the current state of the technology. Likewise, it is not clear how one would build a connectionist system to analyze verbal descriptions of objects in the park, descriptions of the sort originally posed by Hart and Fuller and adapted fairly readily into a classical AI system.

The vehicle-in-the-park system shows some of the limitations of current-day connectionist AI. As with classical approaches, the system designer must restrict the problem domain and in large measure must design the problem around the system instead of the other way around. It is sometimes said that connectionism is more on track in its selection of human attributes than is classical AI, at least to the extent that it is trying to create machine intelligence or model human intelligence. A better view is that connectionism models aspects of human reason that classical AI neglects, but that both classical and connectionist AI are at best small pieces of the puzzle of human reason.

Formalism and Choice of Metaphor

Classical AI and connectionist AI present different views of what sort of machine the mind may be like. By considering different mind-machines, we may develop new ideas in law and jurisprudence. A machine that is intrinsically suited for the open-textured tasks of law provides a better metaphorical description of what judges do than does the judicial slot machine. A machine that is built to draw inexorable conclusions from authoritative premises is in keeping with a model of legal argument that supposes that arguments lead to closure; a fuzzy-logic machine that does not come to a clear answer is in keeping with an open-ended model of argument.

It is worthwhile considering why a formalist version of the mind-machine metaphor appears in both AI and law. Both AI and law are disciplines in which judgment is central. Both are disciplines in which rules are thought to be important. In both disciplines, key thinkers at prestigious universities have promulgated schools of thought under which formalism came to seem inevitable. Both disciplines emphasize verbal and propositional reasoning. AI and law have both aspired to be sciences, though arguably AI is engineering and law is a combination of philosophy, social science, and common sense. AI attempts to model human reason; law, to restrict the operation of human reason in certain social or judicial contexts so as to achieve predictable outcomes.

In both AI and law, as in so many disciplines, the dominant models shape the questions that are and are not asked. New mind-machines may raise new questions. Margaret Jane Radin writes, "For consciousness to exist at all, there must be shared meaning arising out of shared interactions with the world."[28] The machine that is seen as the mind may or may not be embodied or situated in a society. It may or may not be able to imagine and to dream. To the extent that the mind-machine of law is a formalist mind-machine, it hides something essential about being human.

Robots in the Park

All too often you'll find that the difficult technical aspect of a program results from a failure of the program's task to correspond to any real task.
—Philip Agre, *The Dynamic Structure of Everyday Life* (1988)

An interactionist would likely take a very different approach to the problem of how best to enforce Hart and Fuller's mythical ordinance. The interactionist would view the park, and the vehicles and people in it, as a process of situated human activity. He would not attempt to solve in the abstract the question of what counts as a "vehicle" for purposes of the ordinance but instead would set about the practical business of designing a park that does not include unwanted vehicles. To bring the park into compliance with the ordinance, the interactionist might install barricades at all park entrances. These could be simple sawhorse or cone barriers, or the more sophisticated tire traps often seen around college campuses or manufacturing plants. Anything that physically could get by the barricades would not be a vehicle for purposes of the ordinance. This would include bicycles, skateboards, and helicopters. It also would include official cars and trucks (including the war veterans' soon-to-be-a-statue truck) for whom the barricades would be moved, as well as the few drunk or willfully disobedient car drivers who might from time to time ignore the barricades. The latter group would be obvious to the police officers tending the barricades and would receive tickets.

Imagine a vehicle-in-the-park video game. The player is a rookie traffic cop on the beat. Cars, trucks, and motorcycles are trying to drive through the park. The cop can place barricades to stop them or issue tickets if she catches them, but if too many cars enter and exit the park without being ticketed, the cop is dismissed from the police force. Presumably, a Pengi-like program could be written to play this game. Law professors might like to play it, too.

4

Paradigm Shifts

It has been said that AI and jurisprudence each are undergoing Kuhnian paradigm shifts. It has also been said that Kuhnian paradigm shifts are philosophically ill-formed concepts, no more than fancy labels devoid of content that tell us absolutely nothing about the phenomena we observe. Following is a discussion of whether and how the notion of paradigm shift might be at all helpful as a way of looking at changes in AI and law.

Pragmatism

The important thing, it seems to me, is to find a picture that enables us to make sense of the phenomena from within our world and our practice, rather than to seek a God's-Eye View.

—Hilary Putnam, *Representation and Reality* (1988)

Thomas Grey sets forth two prongs of pragmatist commitment: first, that thinking is contextual and situated; and second, that thinking is practical because it is instrumental, or helpful. On the pragmatist view, truth is made, not found. Margaret Jane Radin writes, "truth is inevitably plural, concrete, and provisional," and knowledge is to be found "in the particulars of experience." Traditional dichotomies are to be questioned and dissolved. On the pragmatist view, theory cannot be radically divorced from practice; a change in thinking can mean a change in action, and theory is to be evaluated by how it translates into action. Again, Radin: "Our conceptual schemes and human activity cannot be held apart." If, as Grey suggests, a purpose of the theory game is to get us out of trouble, then one helpful, pragmatic move is to bring our hidden assumptions to light.[1]

An additional pragmatist commitment may be the commitment to situated idealism. Hilary Putnam summarizes this: "Pragmatists do urge that we need to be fallibilistic about our ideals, that ideals are very unlikely ever to be final, that we need to be open and sensitive to the ideals of others and to look for more embracing ideals. But more importantly, pragmatists insist on

the idea of taking ideals seriously. That's what pragmatism is about."[2]
Pragmatism denies a strong fact-value dichotomy. Putnam distinguishes
between this descriptive dichotomy and the prescriptive Is-Ought
dichotomy. But the Is-Ought dichotomy continues to be useful; Karl
Llewellyn spoke of the *temporary* divorce of Is and Ought for purposes of
study, and it is to be understood that ultimately, Is and Ought are points on
a continuum.[3] Indeed, that continuum might be seen in two dimensions.
The first runs between the Is of social practice and the Ought of the extant
law; the second runs between the Is of today and the Ought of possible
futures.

One danger of pragmatism is the tendency of legal pragmatist writers to
say, "Well, it is pragmatically better that A than B." Too-facile use of such
rhetoric becomes a "because I said so" justification, appropriate in authori-
tarian societies or families, but not in modern American jurisprudential
discourse. It is certainly possible not to get caught in this trap, but vigilance
is essential to avoid becoming apologists for the status quo.

A weakness of pragmatism is that although it posits a middle way
between objective formalism and pure subjective preference, it is fairly
unspecific about how that middle way is to be accomplished. Cognitive
science, sociology, and anthropology can help make the middle way more
concrete by showing us more about how we think, theorize, and make
judgments; by revealing hidden assumptions or patterns in our judgments
and providing us with alternatives; and by helping us to understand how the
world in which we are situated acts on us and shapes our choices. AI
research provides a unique opportunity for us better to appreciate how
human reasoning does and does not work. AI provides a testbed for theories of cognition, and a means to sharpen our intuitions about the nature of
human reason as we attempt to design and implement AI systems.

Pragmatism is important to this essay for several reasons. First, pragmatism is one of several schools of thought that supports situated theories of
meaning, antifoundationalism, and antiformalism, which are central to the
discussion in Chapter 3 and underpin the law metaphors developed in
Chapter 5. Second, most critics of Kuhn do not appear to accept pragmatist
commitments,[4] and their critiques in some cases lean on formalist assumptions. Third, pragmatism informs the discussions in Chapter 6 of explanation capability, judging, and rules. Fourth, the notion of a theory-game
developed in the next section, a notion that captures the spirit of the entire
essay, has a nice pragmatist balance to it. It's theory, so we are supposed to
take it seriously; but it's only a game, so we are supposed to have fun with
it and not to believe that it is some sort of revealed truth.

Teach the Children a Map

Every theory aspires to being a logical system but often merely begs the question.
—Ludwik Fleck, *Genesis and Development of a Scientific Fact* (1935)

AI and jurisprudence, as academic disciplines, consist in part of the development of theories. New paradigms presumably include new theories. To talk about paradigm shifts, then, it is helpful to discuss briefly what is meant by a theory. We may consider why people develop theories, how they use those theories, and, finally, what theories are, something that may best be explained metaphorically.

Scientific and Nonscientific Theories

Grey says that we make theories for two reasons: to get out of trouble, and as a form of play. He refers to legal theories, but his description seems about right for many kinds of theories. In our culture, the prototype of an academic theory is probably the scientific theory. In science, theories are a way of making sense of observed data, and of being able to see or extract the data in the first place. Perhaps, then, making sense of the world and making the world out of sense are alternative reasons for theory-making; or perhaps they are just a restatement of Grey's reasons.

The scientific theory serves principally to explain, predict, and control. More generally, a scientific or nonscientific theory may be used to explain, predict, control, interpret, describe, evaluate, conjecture, specify, argue, reassure, choose, and justify. A theory also may serve to spark the creative imagination. Roughly, the more a theory can be used precisely to predict and control the future, the more scientific it is. A theological theory may have great value as an interpretive tool for the past and present yet be of little value in predicting the future or in designing means (e.g., technology, ritual) to cope with that future. Ideally, a scientific theory is quantitative and subject to test by controlled experiment—although there are numerous counterexamples, to the point where the exceptions may swallow the rule.[5]

A continuum of theories might be drawn from the most to the least scientific, or from the most predictive to the most interpretive. Theories from the physical sciences would be the most scientific, followed by theories from the biological sciences. Mechanical, electrical, and chemical engineering theories would also fall on the scientific end of the continuum. Theories of the empirical social sciences, such as experimental psychology and empirical economics, would be more toward the middle of the continuum, although still on the scientific side. Political theory would be closer to the nonscientific end of the continuum, as would anthropology and philosophy. Theories of music, art, literature, and theology would perhaps be the least scientific. One might dispute the placement of particular disciplines along the continuum. Perhaps because of the prestige and legitimacy of science in our culture, we are concerned with how "scientific" our own particular discipline is perceived to be.

It is not altogether clear where to place AI and law on the continuum. Presumably AI belongs somewhere to the scientific side, and law somewhere to the unscientific side. AI seems more like engineering than like pure science. It focuses on building machines, not simply to test theories about nature but as ends in themselves. Regarding the goal of modeling human intelligence, AI may be more like a science, with its models providing the same kind of test of theory provided by computational models in certain branches of physics. But even here, the system being modeled is so poorly understood that such science is at best in its infancy. Law is perhaps more like philosophy or folk wisdom than like social science, and more like social science than like physical science. Its theories describe social interactions and human nature, not physical systems. Although its theories may have some predictive value, they are primarily interpretive; in particular, they are neither quantitative nor subject to test by controlled experiments. A legal academic's theory about justice or jurisprudence probably has little predictive value, at least in any particular case. A lawyer's theory about what a court will do in the case at hand is not the same kind of predictor as a physicist's theory about what a particle will do in the experiment at hand. One's academic bent determines in part how scientific the law appears. An adherent of law and economics may find law more scientific, or at least more amenable to scientific thinking, than does a scholar of law and literature.

From a pragmatist viewpoint, theory cannot be radically separated from practice but makes sense only as applied in context. Typical application contexts for scientific theories, and AI theories, include basic and applied research, commercial manufacture, and teaching. Legal theories of the various sorts to be outlined shortly find application in analogous contexts: in the "research" context of academic discourse; in the "manufacture" contexts of lawyering, including document drafting, negotiation, and litigation, as well as adjudication and legislation; and, of course, in teaching. The coarseness of the analogy between the usages of legal and scientific theories suggests once again that law is less scientific than AI.

Although neither law nor AI is a pure science, both resemble sciences in that they aspire to be rigorous, formal disciplines, placing value on logical thinking, clear rules, and formal theories. Moreover, in both disciplines, new theories are seen, rightly or wrongly, as bringing the disciplines closer to truth. The metaphor of a march of progress is at work. As in science, that march may be a halting, interrupted one, but it is assumed to be more or less forward. In science, forward progress may be measured, inter alia, by technological sophistication, and the same is true in AI. In law, the yardstick is less apparent.

Metametaphors

The term "theory" is used in several different ways in AI and law. In AI, theories may describe the formal structure of various programming methodologies, evaluate the computational complexity of certain tasks, explain the relationship between certain computer programs and the aspects of human intelligence that they model, or specify computational descriptions for certain human intelligence tasks. An AI program embodies a theory about its knowledge domain, a theory of the programming methodology it incorporates, and, in the case of an expert system, a formalist theory of language and meaning. More mundanely, a programmer may have a theory about why a program is failing and how to fix it. In law, legal academics develop theories about what law is, how it derives its legitimacy, how judges should and do decide cases, how law interacts with society, and so forth. Lawyers present their theories of a case to a court. Courts develop theories, which we call doctrine, about how certain areas of the law ought to be dealt with; the American Law Institute develops theories, which we call restatements and model codes, about the same.

A theory may be expressed as a set of formal statements, criteria, or mathematical or verbal formulas. It may include diagrams or pictures and prototypical cases or exemplars from which other cases may be derived. A theory may be implicit; even where an explicit description exists, it seldom tells the whole story. Also, theories may be said to provide categorization schemes, working metaphors, conceptual frameworks, or cognitive models—in other words, ways of seeing the world. Perhaps such a world model is part of a theory; or perhaps it is better to say that a theory constructs a world model in line with its purpose of helping to make sense of the world, and that formulas and formalizations are merely aspects or manifestations of that model.

All this suggests that "theory" is not an altogether precise term, which may seem surprising considering that the prototype of theory is the supposedly rigorous scientific theory. Theory is open-textured. If scientific theory is the core instance, nonscientific theories fall in the penumbra.[6]

One way to understand theory is through metaphor. A metaphor is a way of seeing one thing in terms of another and is inherently inexact. It emphasizes some details and hides others. A metaphor fits some cases more closely than others, giving rise to open texture. If theory provides a metaphor through which we view the world, then a metaphor through which we view theory might be fancifully termed a metametaphor.

If a theory is something that gets us out of trouble, we might say metaphorically that a theory is a map, and the process or activity of doing theory is mapmaking. A map is a guide, an inexact representation of a landscape. It necessarily reduces in size and detail the landscape it represents.[7] It may be available at different scales, giving different degrees of approximation. It may emphasize certain features of the landscape or make certain patterns visible that otherwise would not be. It defines artificial boundaries between areas. It becomes outdated and needs periodic revision to reflect changes in the underlying landscape, new information obtained about an unchanged landscape, or changes in the artificial boundaries. A theory shares these and perhaps other properties of maps.

One can analogize theory to nongeographical maps as well. The mathematical formulas of a theory in the physical sciences create mathematical maps—functions—that represent underlying physical reality. A computer model of a physical or biological system is a sort of map, and the computer graphics output it generates may also be said to be a map. According to the view that the mind is a connectionist network, a theory may be seen as the mathematical function constructed by that network, or perhaps as an approximation to such a function, an approximation whose form may be specified in advance in terms of a mathematical formula.[8] One might picture such a theory as a deformable lattice or hypersurface in a multidimensional representational space. This picture may seem quite abstract. Yet the underlying notion is basically the same as for an ordinary road map: an inexact representation or guide used to make sense of the world.

If a theory is a game, then doing theory is a form of play—"deep play," as Grey puts it.[9] Thanks to Wittgenstein, "game" is the word most famous for indeterminacy. Not only can games include children's games or dice games or even video games, but the boundaries of any given game may be vague as well. Is basketball the same game as one-on-one basketball? If the basketball is punctured and we substitute a soccer ball instead, are we still playing basketball? What if we allow the soccer ball to be kicked, disallow the use of hands, and say that a goal is scored when the ball is kicked against the pole supporting the basketball hoop? What if we replace the basketball hoop and its supporting pole with a large rectangular goal net? And so on. Theories may be similarly indeterminate in their boundaries. It is not clear how much of a theory can be altered before we ought to call it a brand-new theory.

Consider a board game. The rules of the game are specified in the printed instructions; but, as any child knows, the instructions never tell you enough to let you play the game. Your best bet is to find an older kid who already knows how to play and who is willing to teach you. Similarly, the formalized rules of a theory seldom state enough to let the practitioner play the theory-game. Theory cannot be divorced from practice. The rules of the theory-game are a convenient, and necessarily simplified, formalization of the game itself.

A theory-game mirrors practice as play mirrors work. Even if the game is quite complicated, it operates nonetheless in a restricted domain, with restricted consequences. It provides an opportunity for players to try out ideas or judgments, ideally without anyone's getting seriously hurt. This is seen in legal academic writing, and in AI systems designed to work on so-called toy problems.

Other metaphors of theory may be developed. A theory may be seen as a building, and theory-builders as architects.[10] As an activity, theory might be seen as grocery shopping: Pick and choose the items you like, cook them into something nice, and don't worry too much about unwanted leftovers. One might even picture a theory as an AI system, both product of and productive of a mind-machine. A computer program may be seen as an elaborate sort of game; a theory, as an algorithm run by the mind to process sense data into useful results. The problem of theory-making, of modeling the world, is the problem of knowledge representation, which is central to both human and machine cognition.

Virtual Reality

The juxtaposition of the metaphors of theory as game and theory as AI system suggests yet another computer-based metaphor, that of theory seen as virtual reality. "Virtual reality" refers to technology that places one or more human beings in a computer-simulated world. The humans wear video goggles, headphones, electromechanical gloves, and so on and experience the simulated world as their immediate reality. Like AI technologies, virtual-reality technology is in its infancy. However, computer graphics has already demonstrated the ability to produce images that seem strikingly real, as evidenced by any number of recent Hollywood movies. As virtual-reality technology progresses and incorporates advanced graphics capabilities, it may be expected to enable the creation of ever more convincing simulated worlds.

In a sense, virtual reality complements interactionist AI. Interactionism takes the world as its own best model. Intelligence comes about through the interactions of simple creatures in, with, and through the complex world.

Conversely, virtual reality takes an artificial model as the world. Intelligence comes about through the interactions of complex creatures—human beings—in, with, and through the simple world. The thrust of technological development in interactionism is to develop ever more complex creatures. The thrust of technological development in virtual reality is to develop ever more complex environments.

William Gibson's novel *Neuromancer* portrays the ultimate virtual reality. Gibson envisions a future in which all computers are linked in a single gigantic network. Human beings, hooked into the network through telepathic headsets, experience the network as a virtual world, a consensual hallucination called cyberspace. In cyberspace, intelligent agents and the environment are not separate. The computer network provides both. Humans ordinarily experience cyberspace as a world of abstract geometrical forms, like a vast three-dimensional video game. But cyberspace is populated with rogue AIs who can create illusions in the humans who visit there, making cyberspace seem entirely lifelike. Moreover, these AIs can extend their influence into the larger, real world.

Viewed as virtual reality, theory has the power to create experience. Theory is not seen as an instrumentality or a passive backdrop. It is no longer a map to be followed or a game to be played, but a world to be lived, a shared environment in, with, and through which humans interact. Humans shape their theory-world even as it shapes their experience.

Viewed as cyberspace, theory takes on the added dimension of active intelligence. Not only is the theory-world populated by active human agents, but theory itself becomes one or more active agents. The "intelligence" of these agents may be seen in their power to create illusions in human beings and to affect the larger world.

The Turing test supposes that a human observer can reliably distinguish between an intelligent creature and an unintelligent one. Can a human being reliably distinguish between the real world and a hallucinatory virtual one? The answer is usually yes, but not always. Can a human being reliably distinguish those aspects of the world that arise as a consequence of a particular theory from those that would arise under any number of theories? The answer is not clear. The world that theory constructs cannot always be neatly separated from the larger world. Humans may become accustomed to their particular theories, their virtual worlds. At times, the only reality check available is to switch theories and see how the world changes.

Theory and Indeterminacy

That theory is an indeterminate or metaphorically defined term, and that particular theories consist as much in metaphors as in rules, need not be cause for concern. Many words and concepts used in academic discourse, particularly in jurisprudence, are indeterminate yet are nonetheless helpful.

"Law," for example, is indeterminate. It has different connotations in phrases such as common law, statutory law, administrative law, state law, federal law, international law, constitutional law, tax law, corporate law, court of law, the law of the case, law enforcement, law as a matter of social practice, unwritten law, law and economics, law and literature, higher law, God's law, and black-letter law. *A* law is not the same as *the* law, which in turn is not the same as the practice *of* law. Law may be the doctrine that the judge consults, the system that she embodies, the force that she projects. Yet ordinarily, no one suggests that the term "law" be dropped, or that it be dissected and replaced with more precise terms. Law is spoken of as a single entity, a unified whole.

The study of philosophy is in part the study of things for which there is not yet a clear understanding. Given the pervasiveness of open texture and other forms of indeterminacy, it seems likely that attempts to bring rigor and formalism to "theory" and to theories can go only so far. If theory and practice are indeed inseparable, that should come as no surprise after all.

Paradigms and Other Nonsense

To the extent that the Weltanschauungen *approach involves the postulation of such entities* [as paradigms] *it leads to a metaphysically bloated and epistemologically unacceptable picture of scientific theorizing.*
— Frederick Suppe, *The Structure of Scientific Theories* (1977)

It is often the case that something vague is precisely what we want to say.
— Trevor Bench-Capon and Marek Sergot,
"Toward a Rule Based Representation of Open Texture in Law" (1985)

Arguably, the field of artificial intelligence is now undergoing a Kuhnian paradigm shift. Perhaps the shift is from a paradigm centered on classical expert systems to one centered on connectionist systems. Perhaps it is from a paradigm centered on disembodied, unsituated systems to one centered on embodied systems situated in lifelike environments.

Arguably, the field of jurisprudence is now likewise undergoing a Kuhnian paradigm shift. Perhaps the shift is from a paradigm centered on legal formalism to one centered on more situated, contextual approaches to justice. Perhaps the shift is from whatever it is we have now to who knows what. It has been argued that such shifts have taken place in the past, notably with the advent of legal realism and the change in the Supreme Court's jurisprudence in the 1930s.[11]

Of course, for those who do not believe in paradigm shifts, all this is nonsense. . . .

Kuhn and His Critics

To begin with, what is a paradigm, if anything, and why bother with one? Thomas Kuhn coined the term "paradigm" in his classic book *The Structure of Scientific Revolutions*. A paradigm, writ small, is an exemplar for study, a classic problem that serves to instruct students of a science. A paradigm, writ large, is the worldview, or weltanschauung, of a science.[12] In Kuhn's theory, the change in worldview that accompanies a scientific revolution is known as a paradigm shift. Paradigm has a host of other related meanings; Margaret Masterman, a critic sympathetic to Kuhn, found twenty-one different uses of the word "paradigm" in *Scientific Revolutions*. The twenty-one uses include things like a universally recognized scientific achievement, a myth, a philosophy or constellation of beliefs and questions, a textbook or classic work, and an entire scientific tradition. Masterman says that the twenty-one senses of paradigm may be clustered into three groups: metaphysical senses, sociological senses, and artifact or construct senses. She argues that the fundamental sense of "paradigm" is as a construct for puzzle solving. In short, "paradigm" is essentially vague, and therein lies the problem. A term so vague need not be incoherent—indeed, its breadth may be a source of conceptual power—but it does lend itself to misuse. Moreover, critics may easily say that vague terminology hides muddled thinking.

Many have criticized Kuhn. Critics fault Kuhn for, among other things, being imprecise, not painting an accurate picture of science, and providing a theory that cannot be tested empirically. They charge that normal science may not actually occur the way Kuhn says, and that normal science may not be as clearly distinguishable from scientific revolution as Kuhn suggests. Kuhn speaks of the proliferation of schools of thought that presages a revolutionary crisis, yet it may be difficult to tell that proliferation from the proliferation of conflicting theories that may exist during periods of supposedly normal science. Critics also fault Kuhn's relativism. Some have read Kuhn as an extreme relativist who finds changes in scientific theory to be entirely matters of fashion or collective agreement.[13] Some have read him as claiming that different paradigms are wholly incommensurable, a position that is philosophically untenable.[14] Some say that all relativism is more or less the same, and that by rediscovering relativism, Kuhn has simply found true in science what others have found true elsewhere. Still further, Kuhn is criticized for not being original. For instance, he has been accused of stealing many of his ideas from Ludwik Fleck's 1935 book *Genesis and Development of a Scientific Fact*, which was little known at the time Kuhn wrote *Scientific Revolutions*.[15] Finally, critics voice concern that any theory that has become so popularized as has Kuhn's can no longer be regarded as a serious philosophical tool.[16] As if to add credibility to his critics' charges, Kuhn has backed away from his position in *Scientific Revolutions* and has dropped the term "paradigm" altogether.

Critics' charges that Kuhn is too imprecise or too relativist seem for the most part founded in functionalist or objectivist assumptions. In particular, the critics appear to underestimate the pervasiveness of indeterminacy in philosophical discourse and either not to accept or not to grasp fully the implications of the notion that scientists create as much as observe experimental reality. In other words, the critics do not see the middle way. To be fair, much of the criticism comes from adherents of analytic philosophy and predates the 1980s, when Putnam, respected among analytic philosophers, made the strong case for the failure of functionalism. Still, it is frustrating to find that Kuhn and his critics, Masterman excepted, often appear to be talking past one another. Read in light of philosophies that recognize alternatives to the objective-subjective dichotomy, Kuhn makes a great deal of sense. Unfortunately, to give a full justification of these contentions or a point-by-point rebuttal to Kuhn's critics would require another essay.

On Kuhn's originality, Masterman has this to say: "The widely held popular views that Kuhn is not really saying anything new or that in so far as he is a philosopher at all, his views are essentially the same as Feyerabend's . . . all these judgments can be shown, from actual examination of Kuhn's text, to be false. It is, in fact, the very differences between Kuhn's image of science . . . and all other philosophies of science . . . which is causing Kuhn's book to be so widely read."[17] Clearly, Kuhn is not the only thinker to question more traditional views of scientific progress. But he has become the best known. His clarity of exposition and his accessible, narrative writing style, a style not commonly associated with philosophical discourse, have probably contributed as much to his wide readership as has his iconoclasm. Kuhn's metaphors of scientific revolutions as gestalt flips and of science as society provide intuitively plausible understandings of complex phenomena.[18] Perhaps most important, Kuhn says elegantly what many people have felt to be true all along.[19]

Critics' charges that Kuhn's popularization has robbed his theory of whatever philosophical usefulness it may once have had contain a great deal of truth. "Paradigm" has become a buzzword used whenever someone wants people to jump on his or her bandwagon. A blatant example is the recent use of "paradigm shift" by a Bush administration aide, James P. Pinkerton, to describe what he sees as a new Republican political tradition sweeping the nation.[20] Examples may be found in legal scholarship as well, as Peter Teachout dryly observes:

> To pull off a successful paradigm shift, you must go through four basic steps. First, you have to paint a melancholy view of the world around us. . . . Second, you have to identify the one thing—usually, the key cultural notion—that has made the world such a miserable place. This is called identifying the corruptive paradigm. . . . Sometimes [legal] scholars . . . get into heated arguments over which particular cultural notion is the corruptive paradigm. . . . [But all] you have to do is say that the particular paradigm you picked as the corruptive paradigm forms just the center of a whole wicked constellation of values and attitudes, and that it is the whole constellation that has gotten us into so much trouble. Then everyone will be satisfied. The third step . . . is to identify a new paradigm—the saving paradigm. . . . The fourth and final step is imagining how nice the world would be if the new constellation were put in place of the old one.[21]

"Paradigm" is likewise used to discredit opposing viewpoints. The argument goes, If you don't see that I am correct, it is just because you are blinded by your obsolete paradigm. With such widespread misuse of his theory, perhaps it is no wonder that Kuhn has retreated into what one reporter called "stoic obscurity."[22]

Salvaging "Paradigm"

> *Our deepest clashes aren't even clashes over principles; they are clashes over visions. "Visions" is a messy term—philosophers don't like to use terms like vision. But generally one's principles, rules, and judgments about individual cases hang together, however loosely and with whatever inconsistencies, in something one might call a moral vision or a moral ideal.*
>
> —Hilary Putnam, remarks in the afterword of *Symposium on the Renaissance of Pragmatism in American Legal Thought* (1990)

To dismiss the idea of a paradigm simply because it is essentially vague or because it has become popularized is to throw out the good with the bad. Paradigms can provide a helpful way of unifying thinking about a number of seemingly disparate phenomena, and paradigm shifts, a useful way of interpreting change in various disciplines.

The term "paradigm" includes or connotes a broad range of ideas regarding conceptual coherence. It suggests the fundamental importance of shared metaphors, conceptual categories, and cognitive models; of recognized exemplars; of standard texts and codified dogma; of common norms, practices, and goals—in short, the importance of a coherent conceptual framework or language to any science or, by extension, to any discipline. It suggests that such conceptual coherence is linked to a corresponding institutional or sociological coherence. It also connotes the notion of conceptual change as marked by revolutionary crises that punctuate longer periods of slow evolution or equilibrium. Upon the resolution of such crises, previously unexplained anomalies fall into place in a new conceptual framework. Paradigm also carries the notion of incommensurability of old and new paradigms. Incommensurability gives rise to the phenomenon of "talking past one another," in which two parties to an argument seem to differ so totally in their assumptions that it is as though they are holding two different conversations. The notion of gestalt flipping as a metaphorical description of paradigm shift carries with it the idea that although old and new paradigms may be incommensurable, they are not radically so; one can learn to adopt both positions, although not simultaneously. That the description is metaphorical implies that it highlights some aspects of paradigm incommensurability and hides others, and that there are other ways of coming at incommensurability such as that of limiting cases; for example, Newtonian mechanics is sometimes seen as a limiting case of the quantum mechanical view of the world. Perhaps most important, paradigm suggests that scientific knowledge, like other knowledge, is psychologically and sociologically contingent. It points to the act of faith at the heart of science.

Closely linked to that act of faith is the notion of entrenchment of the reigning paradigm. "Entrenchment" is used here to capture the idea that people lock into a particular worldview or mindset and may be unable to see things from a fundamentally different perspective. Moreover, they may be unwilling to try. The result is a resistance to change.[23] The resistance is for the most part a good thing; scientists ought to be skeptical of radically new ideas because most such ideas turn out to be wrong and because limited resources would be wasted if every such idea were pursued. Moreover, maintaining one's accustomed perspective is a matter of efficiency. If scientists stopped to question the basics of theory at every step, they would not accomplish anything. Nonetheless, too much skepticism can be counterproductive, and the line between healthy skepticism and dogmatism can be a fine one. Keeping in mind the limitations of a theory or a worldview requires considerable perspective and self-criticism. One may fail to question one's assumptions not for reasons of prudence or efficiency, but because such questioning makes one uncomfortable. Moreover, even a scientist who genuinely wants to entertain a radically new viewpoint may be unable to do so. It is difficult to unlearn what one has known for years. Subconsciously, it becomes difficult or impossible to break free of an existing paradigm, even when one consciously attempts to take a new approach. Finally, for a new viewpoint to emerge, someone has to develop it, and that is no mean feat. The biggest reason for entrenchment may simply be that human beings are not that smart.[24]

The power of having the single word "paradigm" is that it provides conceptual unity, precisely because it calls so much to mind at once. Arguably, a reductionist approach that tries to treat exemplars, incommensurability, entrenchment, and so forth as distinct, rather than as aspects of a single coherent phenomenon, loses something essential.[25] For instance, by recognizing a paradigm, one may be better able to interpret what might otherwise seem like an unexplained resistance to change. Because entrenchment is an essential component of a paradigm, one may expect that academic institutions with shared exemplars and norms will tend to resist fundamental change and, in particular, will tend to resist the asking of questions that do not fit an established worldview. Received wisdom will become reified ideology. Furthermore, as a practical matter, debate that goes to the heart of that ideology is likely to result in the parties to the debate simply talking past one another. By realizing this tendency in advance, one may save time, frustration, or both. In general, the different meanings of paradigm are facets of the whole, which must be grasped as a whole to be appreciated fully. The cluster of concepts is more powerful than any one alone.[26]

Undoubtedly there are other ways of getting at some of the same notions that are bound up in the concept of paradigm. For instance, talking past one another is a phenomenon that may be understood in terms of analogy to a fundamental political or religious disagreement. The argument here is simply that the idea of a paradigm provides one useful way of viewing this and other related phenomena.

The concepts of paradigm and theory overlap quite a bit but are not identical. Like a theory, a paradigm is something through which one sees the world, and the paradigm fits the world only inexactly. Like a theory, a paradigm is more than a list of rules or stated exemplars; it seldom can be fully communicated by explicit, written-down knowledge. Like a theory, a paradigm may be seen at many levels of generality or specificity. But unlike a theory, a paradigm also connotes a community of people who share a vision, and not just the vision itself. Also, theories may evolve, but paradigms shift. The connotations of gestalt flipping and incommensurability are absent from the word "theory." The connotations of entrenchment and of an act of faith are likewise missing.

Because paradigm is an indeterminate concept, categorizing something as a paradigm is not a cut-and-dried process. The boundaries of any given paradigm are themselves indeterminate, at least open-textured if not essentially vague. Telling the difference between a paradigm and a theory, or between normal science and revolutionary science, is a matter of interpretation. Because "theory" and even "science" are also indeterminate terms (Is a molecular geneticist in the same science as an animal behavior biologist? Are any two molecular genetics laboratories practicing quite the same science?), the room for interpretation is quite considerable. If we adopt the metaphor that a theory is a game, a new theory represents a modification of the rules, and a scientific revolution or paradigm shift is a change to an entirely new game. If we adopt the metaphor that a theory is a map or guide, theory may be seen as a tool applied to practice, and a paradigm includes or subsumes the entire theory-practice totality. The cluster of concepts that constitute a paradigm reinforces the notion that scientific theory and scientific practice are inseparable.

Given the indeterminacy of Kuhn's terminology, coupled with critics' charges that his theory does not accurately depict the history of science, Kuhn's theory may best be understood as interpretive.[27] On this view, Kuhn provides a narrative or stylized version of scientific change rather than a literal description. His theory is useful to explain and perhaps to control the present, but not so much to predict the future; in particular, it is not especially useful for predicting a scientific revolution or for predicting what a postrevolutionary paradigm may look like. Indeed, an observer may be unable except in retrospect to tell that a paradigm shift has in fact occurred.[28] To the extent that this is true, Kuhn's critics are correct in saying that definitive predictions of imminent paradigm shifts are likely to be little more than attempts to win support for favored positions.

Even to the extent Kuhn's theory is valid, it is sometimes said that it is valid for science only. Kuhn himself questions the extension of his theory beyond science. Arguably, however, *paradigms tell us less about science than they do about people*. Science is not a discipline that is "out there" waiting for philosophers of science objectively to discover how it is and is not done. Science, or for that matter any discipline, is constructed by and constructive of people. Kuhn presents a way of understanding this. Alternatively, the idea of a paradigm shift provides a metaphor in which change in other disciplines may be understood in terms of Kuhn's portrayal of scientific change. The metaphor seems especially apt in the case of rational or rigorous disciplines such as AI and law.

Paradigms, AI, and Law

We return to the question that began this section: What value, if any, is the notion of a paradigm shift in AI or in law? The short answer is, not much. Arguably, the question of whether we are undergoing a paradigm shift is ill-formed. What constitutes a paradigm is a matter of interpretation. Determining when a paradigm has shifted requires perspective that is unlikely to be attainable without the benefit of considerable hindsight. Even the boundaries of the disciplines of law and AI are not determinate. It may be unclear whether to include certain kinds of computer technology under the rubric of AI. It may be unclear whether to include only legal academia, or also the courts. Finally, perhaps neither law nor AI is yet at the stage of normal science. Law and AI each consist of many schools of thought, and perhaps both disciplines are better seen as being at the preparadigm stage, the stage of alchemy before the rise of chemistry.[29]

The short answer, however, is not the complete answer. For all its vagueness, Kuhn's theory may provide helpful insights. By treating various interpretations under Kuhn's theory as equally valid, rather than attempting to select one best interpretation, we may learn something from each. Thus, for example, rather than asking whether classical and connectionist AI are different paradigms, we may ask what we can learn by treating them as different paradigms, and alternatively, what we can learn by treating them as belonging to different specialties within the same larger discipline and paradigm. Similarly, there may be something to be learned by treating law and economics, critical legal studies, and feminist legal theory as different paradigms or, alternatively, as the competing schools of thought that prefigure a revolutionary crisis.

Perhaps the main thing to be learned is perspective. Kuhn's theory helps us appreciate the contingent nature of what seems at times to be objective truth. Likewise, it helps us appreciate the tendency of a dominant paradigm to become entrenched, and for our own thinking to be molded by the dominant paradigm. The theory helps us to recognize when we are talking past each other and to cultivate patience for trying, as best we can, to do something about it while at the same time realizing that try as we might, we may ultimately be unable to see the other side. In short, by thinking of ourselves as being in a paradigm, we may be more open-minded and more humble.

What is striking about Kuhn's theory is that it arises in and prototypically applies to science, a discipline traditionally thought to be rigorous, formal, incremental in its advance, and above all characterized by reasoned dispute over objectively verifiable hypotheses. The theory shows that even in this supposedly rational discipline, entrenchment occurs and fundamental change requires acts of faith. To the extent that AI and law pattern themselves after the traditional myth of objective science and derive prestige and legitimacy therefrom, Kuhn's theory undermines that prestige and legitimacy by destabilizing the myth. Arguably, that is all to the good.

Therapy

Psychotherapy is an attempt to bring about a paradigm shift of sorts for the patient. It is a process of letting go of one's past and preconceptions. In therapy the patient seeks to reconnect with her feelings and memories, both past and present, and may seek explanations, or justifications, for her behavior. She attempts to integrate old experiences and knowledge in a new conceptual framework, a framework more helpful than her previous framework.

One aspect of a psychotherapist's role is to offer her patient alternative models of self and world. Call them tools, strategies, theories; they enable the patient to reinvent herself. For therapy to be effective, the theory-practice connection must be strong. The therapist's teachings are not understood except through integration into daily experience. They are applied in context, through situated judgment. They very much fit Grey's notion of theory: The new strategies are games. The patient cannot know whether or how well they will work unless she allows herself to play with them and see what comes up. As she does so, she changes the games and makes them her own.

Besides offering substantive theories of self and behavior, the therapist offers procedures (strategies, techniques, games) for breaking out of accustomed thought patterns. The therapist may employ visualization, guided imagery, bodywork, or other techniques to help the patient bypass her ordinary patterns of thought. The therapist may encourage the patient to verbalize what is going on inside her. This may be difficult, because the act of reporting verbally on a feeling may cause the patient to "disconnect" from that feeling, bringing her to a state in which she intellectualizes about the feeling rather than being immediately and fully aware of the feeling and its associated body sensations. The patient needs to learn to bridge the gap between the two modalities of thought, to connect verbal theory with emotional practice.[30]

In AI and law, and perhaps in science as well, a paradigm shift may be seen as a healing conceptual breakthrough, much like a therapeutic breakthrough. However, a discipline must play the role of its own therapist. As a result, theorists may seek help from friends or books, but ultimately they must spend a great deal of time groping about in the dark until something turns up. Moreover, a discipline's paradigm shift does not come in a single moment and may not be perceptible for years. However, any individual practitioner of the discipline may immediately perceive a breakthrough as a flash of insight or a gestalt flip, just as a patient in therapy might do. The breakthrough may be small or large and may prove to be illusory, but it is nonetheless exciting to experience. Also, like a patient in therapy, the individual practitioner may look to laughter as an indicator of progress. Often-times in therapy, laughter marks a moment of self-realization. So, too, in AI or in law, our ability to laugh at ourselves helps to keep us grounded, aware of our own situation and our limits, pragmatic about our theory-games.

5

Law as Mind-Machine

Consider for example, the definitions of life and mind given by Herbert Spencer: correspondence of an inner order with an outer order. It implies there is an inner order and an outer order, and that the correspondence consists in the fact that the terms in one order are related to one another as the terms or members of the other order are connected within themselves. The correspondence is like that of various phonographic records to one another; but the genuine correspondence of life and mind with nature is like the correspondence of two persons who "correspond" in order to learn each one of the acts, ideas and intents of the other one, in such ways as to modify one's own intents, ideas and acts, and to substitute partaking in a common and inclusive situation for separate and independent performances. If the organism merely repeats in the series of its own self-enclosed acts the order already given without, death speedily closes its career.
—John Dewey, *Experience and Nature* (1929)

The jurisprudential literature is replete with metaphors of law. Felix Cohen and Duncan Kennedy describe law as a force field. The saddle points created by the boundary between two such fields are analogous to points where the law is unsettled. Where the gradient of the force field is steep, the law is clear. Ronald Dworkin poses law as a chain novel. Laurence Tribe invokes quantum mechanical and relativistic metaphors. Glenn Harlan Reynolds proposes the metaphor of constitutional law as a dynamical system evolving according to the laws of mathematical chaos. There are potentially many others.

AI can provide metaphors of law. E. Donald Elliott has proposed that the common law be viewed as an AI learning machine in which "limited, local intelligence of judges [is used] to build a global intelligence in the system as a whole. Thereby, the law may hope to be wiser than the individuals who make it."[1] Legal expert systems suggest the metaphor of law as a classical AI system. The limits of such expert systems are, as we have seen, in some ways analogous to the limits of a rule-based conception of law in that both offer poor representations of indeterminacy.

Newer AI approaches provide new, possibly more robust metaphorical conceptions of law. Law may be seen as an unsupervised connectionist network, as a hybrid classical-connectionist AI system, or as an embodied, situated robot intelligence. The deformable lattice as a visual representation of the mathematical function constructed by a connectionist law network suggests yet another metaphor of law—law as a quilt.

What is striking in AI and law today, as well as in philosophy and perhaps in other disciplines, is the abandonment of rule-based or formalist approaches, with their image of the detached Cartesian observer and the corresponding disembodied mind-machine metaphor, and the adoption instead of approaches that stress the embodied, situated, pragmatic nature of knowledge and cognition. Related is the notion of emergent properties, a notion that is basic to connectionist and interactionist systems, and that in a broad sense also underlies the notion of holistic or contextual knowledge stressed by jurisprudential movements such as critical feminist jurisprudence and critical jurisprudence of scholars of color, movements that tend to see the consequences of a legal system as best described in terms of the action of the system as a whole rather than in terms of the classical liberal picture of discrete acts by autonomous actors in a neutral and passive context. The metaphors of law as connectionist system, embodied robot, and quilt attempt to capture some of these significant qualities of law.

Resonance

The connectionist metaphor to be developed further on uses the concept of resonance. In physics, resonance describes the behavior of a mechanical or electrical system that oscillates when driven in phase by a periodic power source at the proper frequency. The resonant system amplifies the strength of the power source; the source repeatedly gives small-amplitude "kicks" to the system at the proper times until the system's oscillation amplitude becomes very large and the oscillations take on a life of their own.

Resonance may also occur between two coupled oscillators. The oscillations of the first oscillator set the second one in motion. However, once resonance is in full swing, it is not possible to say that the second oscillator is merely responding to the input of the first, or conversely that the two oscillators have switched roles so that the second one is now driving the motion of the first. Rather, the two oscillators become an inextricably coupled system, with energy moving back and forth throughout. Cause and effect blur in such a system.

Metaphorically, in law, resonance is a way of seeing the relationship between theory and practice, or between law and society. Law and society resonate like a pair of damped, driven, coupled mechanical oscillators. One amplifies the other; the whole is greater than the sum of the parts. If one shifts too far, it tends to pull the other along while the other tends to pull it back. If the system is driven too hard, smooth oscillations break down and mathematical chaos sets in. For example, in the school desegregation cases, the courts raced ahead of prevailing norms, which resulted in social upheaval. The resonance model does not say that such chaos is bad or good, only that it will occur. The resonance model embodies the seeming paradox that law is simultaneously conservative and dynamic.

The concept of resonance occurs in the connectionist AI literature as well, in the work of Stephen Grossberg. Grossberg develops unsupervised learning networks based on what he calls adaptive resonance theory (ART). Central to the operation of such networks is the idea of a resonance between two subsystems. The first subsystem recognizes input patterns; the second provides expectations based on previously learned patterns. When the first subsystem is presented with input similar to previously seen input, it triggers the second subsystem. The second subsystem responds by actively reconstructing the recognized input pattern, which it then feeds back to the first subsystem, reinforcing the input. The resulting resonance acts to "keep signals active after the inputs cease."[2] More generally, the two systems interact in such a way as to enable the network as a whole to recognize changes to input, and to resist or respond to those changes appropriately according to their significance.[3] The stability of the adaptive resonance in the face of perturbations to input mirrors metaphorically the analogous stability in physical or electrical resonances.

Law as Connectionist Network

It will be recalled that a connectionist network is in some sense a curve-fitting or function-approximation machine, where the curve to be fit may be too complex to be specified as an explicit mathematical formula. The network constructs an approximation that may likewise be too complex to specify, short of writing out the equations for the entire network. One may imagine that it might be useful to have an approximation that is simple enough to be represented as an explicit, straightforward formula. Such a formula provides a simplified representation both of the curve to be fit and of the network's approximation to that curve. That is to say, it provides a map—a theory.

The better a theory, the more helpful it is for some purpose. One simplified curve fit may be more helpful than another because it represents a closer fit to the actual form of the underlying function. Alternatively, it may be a closer fit to some desired state of the underlying function and may be used to provide an exemplar for retraining the network so that the network sees the world according to the desired theoretical view. As the network attempts to seek a best fit to the theory, the network function approximation changes to conform itself to the theory.

As an example, suppose a psychotherapy patient's mind is viewed as a connectionist network. The patient may have an inadequate theory, or no theory at all, of himself—that is, no explicit form in which to express the function constructed by his mind. The therapist provides the patient with such a theory. The therapist's theory may be more realistic, providing a better approximation of the actual workings of the patient's mind, or may be more helpful, providing an approximation of the way the patient's mind might work differently, a goal for the patient to emulate. Most likely, the theory will be some of both. Over the course of therapy, as the patient plays with the theory, the patient's mind-function will reshape itself to conform to the theory; at the same time, the theory will evolve to fit more closely the patient's mind-function in a give-and-take between theory and practice.

Now imagine law as a huge adaptive resonance network.[4] The judges and other legal actors are the nodes of the network; the published case reports and statutes, teaching in the law schools, continuing education courses and learning on the job, and the informal and formal oral communications among the members of the legal community are the connections between nodes; the cases and statutes themselves are the patterns presented to and learned by the network. For instance, cases are exemplars, sampled data that train the network; the network attempts from these samples to construct a smooth best-fit function that constitutes its model of the domain, which is the domain of societal interactions subject to law, or in other words, more or less the society as a whole. Established precedent corresponds to very stable learned patterns or prototypes. The network of the law responds to significant changes in the society it serves while at the same time providing stability against insignificant or disruptive changes.

The network metaphor fits neither the image of law as the application of prespecified rules to objective facts nor the image of law as the sum of subjective preferences of individual judges. In the network metaphor, no single autonomous actor or single rule determines the outcome in a lawmaking or judicial decisionmaking act. The knowledge of the system is stored as much in its interconnections as in its nodes, and the properties of the system are emergent as much as they are local. This differs somewhat from a current-day connectionist AI system, in which virtually *none* of the system's behavior is visible in any individual node. In the law network, nodes (legal actors) are themselves intelligent. In connectionist systems of the future, it may be that the "nodes" will themselves be intelligent subsystems, so that the parallels between the two will be closer. Although the network has a hierarchical structure, it has no truly central control; the powerful legal actors such as the Supreme Court respond to the network as much as they control it.

The law that is the network could be the common law, constitutional law, Anglo-American law, even all of law. That law may be mapped metaphorically onto the patterns stored in the ART network or the network itself. The patterns are the cases, statutes, or rules. The network is the law personified. The metaphor is itself indeterminate, perhaps because "law" is essentially vague.

Underlying the metaphor of law as a connectionist network is the mind-machine metaphor. The mind-machine metaphor perspective tends to hide the moral and ethical aspects of law, as well as the question of the source or sources of the law's legitimacy. It focuses on how the law works and de-emphasizes questions of how it got to be that way or whether it ought to be so.

The Network Function

Metaphorically, the law network constructs a mathematical function that represents an approximation to the society. A new theory of a desired state of the law can be used, as in the case of individual therapy, to retrain the network, and again as in individual therapy, that theory will evolve as the network evolves, in a give-and-take between theory and practice. The network metaphor sees law as a gigantic mind-machine attempting constantly to learn and to improve itself. Law learns slowly, however, because its stable, resonant learned patterns resist change. The tension between the needs for stability and plasticity parallels the design problem in ART networks.[5]

The function constructed by the law network may be represented as a manifold in an n-dimensional space where n is a large number. The many dimensions correspond to the classification or categorization dimensions by which the law discriminates among cases. The number of dimensions may vary according to the particular area of law. Thus legal space is not of a fixed number of dimensions.

The law network function is not necessarily single-valued. For example, conflicting precedents can give rise to bifurcations or multivalued sections of the function. Indeed, the function may be fuzzy-valued in places. Also, it may exhibit sharp gradients and steep higher-order derivatives corresponding to the points of unsettled law that the force field metaphor represents as the border between two opposing fields. Singularities may arise in the function due to outlying cases. Even where the function is smooth, it is a best fit rather than an interpolation and may not actually go through its sample points. That is, it may come to differ from the cases that originally went into its formation. In general, the function is extraordinarily complicated.

Rules and Theories
as Approximations to the Function

To make tractable the complicated function that is law, legal actors must work with legal theories, approximations to the function. As with the therapy patient, who needs a theory of her own network in order to understand it and to retrain it, so too, the law needs theories of itself. This leads to a self-reference. In therapy and in law, the network is both subject and object, both student and thing studied. The patient's theory of her mind becomes part of her mind, and theories of law become essential parts of the law.

In particular, legal rules may be seen as theories in the function-approximation sense developed here. They are simplifications, easily stated approximations to the shape of the law in some local region of legal space. They may approximate the law network function either as it already is (as in most judge-made rules) or as certain legal actors wish it to be (as in statutes, regulations, and many Supreme Court decisions). The traditional dichotomy between rules and cases is resolved in this picture. Legal rules emerge or are posed as generalized cases, where the generalization is of the robust, open-textured sort at which connectionist networks excel.[6]

Rule indeterminacies are immediately apparent in this picture. The open texture of rules inheres in the fact that they are approximations, and moreover in the network's ability to generalize from such approximations. Core-penumbra effects arise where the rule approximation fits well in a local area and poorly elsewhere; the more sharply and rapidly varying the function, the more difficult it may be to obtain a good fit. The indeterminacy of time comes about from the fact that rules are perforce developed to approximate the law at a given instant in time; but the law continues to evolve, so that at some later time, its shape may have changed sufficiently to no longer fit the approximation well. Deliberate vagueness may come about when a legislature wishes the law to evolve of its own accord, rather than to constrain such evolution by providing a clear exemplar. In that case, the legislature provides an approximation that may be underspecified in some dimensions or that may provide only a fuzzy fit to the existing shape of the law, providing ample room for the law to develop on its own. Conflicting interpretations may arise when two different formulas provide equally reasonable, yet distinct, approximations to the law network function; this appears quite likely given the extreme complexity and high dimensionality of the function. Finally, essential vagueness obtains when a rule attempts to approximate a very broad area of legal space and in so doing necessarily achieves a very loose fit.

Theories and rules, being approximations, inevitably do not match exactly the underlying law. Such inexact matching may be seen as useful simplification or dangerous distortion, or as something in between. Rules and theories may be seen as attempts to codify the truth or as attempts to shape the truth or, again, as something in between. The quality and useful-ness of the rule depend in part on the shape of the law itself. Where the law function is smooth and not rapidly changing, the fit between the law and the rule-approximation may be extremely good. Where the law function is not varying rapidly in time, a rule may prove quite durable.

Any legal actor's mind may itself be viewed as a network. Each such network contains not only information about that actor's role as a node in the larger network of the law but also some microcosm of the law itself, a theory that reflects in miniature the function of the entire network. An actor in a powerful position in the network may be able to influence the network to conform more to the actor's personal theory of how the law should be. But such influence is constrained by the rest of the law network, and the actor's theory is seen to be as much or more a product of the actor's position in that larger network as of any independent or objective observa-tion powers the actor traditionally might be thought to possess.

Time Evolution and the Quasi-Static Approximation

The law network function is assumed to vary in time.[7] Several factors drive the function's time evolution. First, any given case at bar changes the function. The network, like an unsupervised connectionist network, is always in learning mode, simultaneously responding to the stimulus and learning. The network recognizes the input pattern of the case and attempts to classify it with known similar patterns. Yet, depending on the network's sensitivity to differences, certain features of the case may be perceived as different from those already known to the system, perhaps causing the function to change. The change may be slight, as where a particular surface of that function deforms slightly and locally, or may be dramatic, as where a new bifurcation in the function develops or a classification dimension of the local legal space comes into being or collapses. In particular, a controversial high-court case may substantially deform the function.

At the same time as the given case is interacting with the network, other cases are doing so as well. The cases in the system act asynchronously and sometimes at odds with one another. Moreover, the cases interact with promulgated rules. The rules serve to shape the way incoming cases are viewed. The cases may be viewed as bottom-up inputs, the rules as top-down, once more in analogy with ART. The shape of the function being approximated changes through a court's attempt in a particular case to apply its rule-approximation of that function. New statutes and regulations likewise change the function.

Changes in the courts also change the function, especially changes on the Supreme Court. New justices and judges act and respond differently as network nodes. They approximate the network function differently from their predecessors, or seek to change its shape altogether.

Traditionally, a common law judge is supposed to be a detached observer who applies and does not make the law. The law network metaphor suggests that law is made as it is applied. The network metaphor and traditional pictures may be reconciled by invoking a quasi-static approximation. Assuming that the network function changes sufficiently slowly, the law function's rate of change over time (that is, its time derivative) may be taken as approximately zero for purposes of the case at bar. The court then assumes that its decision changes the law, if at all, only in subsequent cases, not as part and parcel of the decisionmaking process at hand. Where the law is well settled, or where a change in the law is applied only prospectively, the quasi-static approximation is likely to be valid. Indeed, the stability properties of the law's adaptive resonance suggest that a case sufficiently similar to past cases will be considered an insignificant change and will change the shape of the function only slightly, if at all. But where the law is in flux, or where the adversary system's traditional model of the passive judge is inadequate, the quasi-static approximation may break down.

Law as Robot

A final factor in the law function's time evolution is societal change. Technological, political, economic, and cultural changes all shape the law function, both directly and through their effects on individual and public theories about that function. A limitation in the network metaphor appears here, however. Society not only drives changes in law but is driven by them. Society resonates with law.

More generally, law is constructive of and constructed by the world. But the image of law as a connectionist network is an image of law as a disembodied, unsituated intelligence. The disembodied intellect may be a Cartesian objective observer of society; or if we suppose that all the law "knows" is a collection of patterns learned from experience, and that there are no "real" constraints on the law's function, the disembodied intellect may be a radically subjective super–legal realist. Both views take society as a given. Neither view is consistent with the philosophy that cognition, intelligence, and meaning depend on real-world context and interaction.

A Connectionist Robot

An expanded version of the connectionist-network metaphor addresses this limitation. Imagine that the network has a body, allowing it to act on as well as to perceive society. It would be in keeping with the AI metaphor to imagine that body as a robot body. It would be more in keeping with the size of law and the nature of its interaction with society to imagine law's body as society itself; the law would act as the brain of the societal body in much the same way that HAL, the computer in the movie *2001: A Space Odyssey*, controlled the spaceship in which it was embedded.[8] On this view, the spaceship—society—is the robot body. Or perhaps the body is those aspects of society that law controls and to which it responds. The line between society as body and society as environment blurs. Even the notion of law as a separate brain is potentially misleading, as it implies a sharp brain-body dichotomy. Perhaps the mind of law is distributed throughout the body of society.

Like the network metaphor, the robot metaphor is open to different interpretations regarding what aspects of law (common law, constitutional law, etc.) are to be mapped metaphorically, and what they correspond to in the robot. In the robot metaphor, the law may be seen as the knowledge that the robot has or as the robot's connectionist-network brain. These are the same mappings as before, except that in the latter case, which is the law personified, law is viewed as an actor rather than as a passive landscape. Additionally, law may be seen as being the robot's output or, in other words, as the law in action as it shapes society. Finally, the entire law-society machine may be called law as well.

A problem with this metaphor is that one might expect a robot to be capable of planning and reasoning, serial tasks not performed by current-day connectionist AI systems, including ART. One way to deal with this problem is to suppose that the law robot's machine-mind incorporates advanced connectionist or hybrid technologies that have yet to be developed. Another way is to observe that at least when considered as a whole, law is not ordinarily thought of as performing such tasks anyway. It is difficult to picture law in the same way we picture HAL, as a conscious, self-aware entity. The law gives answers but has no awareness.

An Interactionist Robot

Consider two interpretations of the law or law-society robot metaphor: If the robot is viewed in terms of the usual mind-machine metaphor, then law is seen as the locus of the robot's intelligence, and society, as the robot's nonintelligent body-environment. Alternatively, an interactionist view may be adopted, in which case the entire law-society system is seen as giving rise to an intelligence process. In the interactionist version of the robot metaphor, the law-robot may be supposed to be one of Brooks's machines, a robot whose complex and relatively reliable behavior emerges from the contributions of simpler, possibly unreliable or antagonistic components communicating through the medium of the world. Or the law-robot may be supposed to be the embodied, situated connectionist machine already discussed, reinterpreted from an interactionist standpoint.

The interactionist version of the robot metaphor denies law and society the roles of autonomous agents. Law is not seen as actor and society as acted upon, or vice versa; rather, law and society interact with and through one another, with no clear boundary separating actors from action. The intelligence associated with the law-society system is not unitary or centralized and, in particular, is not identified with the overtly legal organs of society: the judiciary, the legislature, the executive branch. Rather, law and society together exhibit an intelligence that cannot be uniquely associated with either one alone.[9]

The interactionist metaphor emphasizes the routine, unspoken aspects of law. At the same time, the metaphor masks the verbal, problem-solving aspects traditionally associated with law. Brooks's robots, after all, lack explicit mechanisms to ensure that their paramount purpose—to serve and protect humans—will be carried out.

Of course, explicit control mechanisms do not always work as planned. Isaac Asimov's classic robot stories portray robots as autonomous, not-quite-human beings caught up in the conflicting demands of deeply ingrained rules. The stories often revolve around situations in which the rules (the three laws of robotics) conflict with one another or break down altogether, situations in which human beings must be called in to set things right. The stories illustrate that a balance of mind and world, of central directive and situated interaction, is needed in law as in robotics.

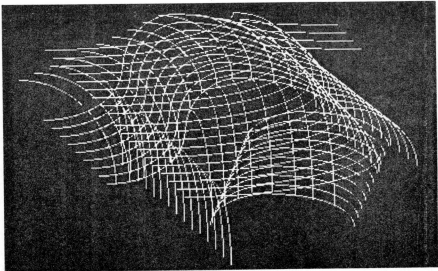

FIGURE 1

Quilting

The fabric of thought before us . . . is something we seek to discern, so that we may truly know what it is, but it is also something that we inevitably help to create as we strive (in accordance with our obligation of fidelity to law) to make the statute a coherent, workable whole.

—Lon Fuller, "Positivism and Fidelity to Law—
A Reply to Professor Hart" (1958)

One may picture the function constructed by the law network as a hypersurface in a multidimensional space. The image that comes to mind might be that of a computer graphics display of an intricate curved surface webbed by grid lines, an image familiar from television and movies. (See Figure 1.) On this view the network function is an abstraction, simply a set of points. But another view of that same function is as a fabric. The grid lines become the threads; the maxima and minima of the function, folds and creases. The abstract point set becomes a physical entity.

The fabric is to be imagined as being stretched taut. An impulse disturbance propagates throughout the fabric according to the physical laws of wave motion. Likewise, in the law, a sudden deformation of the lattice in one place can be expected to have ripple effects elsewhere. This kind of ripple effect is perhaps not inconsistent with the network metaphor, but it is not emphasized by that metaphor, either.

To take the fabric metaphor a step further, imagine the law as a patch-work quilt. The grid is the outline of squares; the threads within each square create a dense, richly colored texture; the whole, though composed of many disparate patches, embodies a coherent design. The quilt metaphor is in some respects like a two-dimensional (or n-dimensional) version of Dworkin's chain novel. But the quilt communicates in pictures, not words. The viewer understands the quilt in a single gestalt rather than focusing on the most recent addition as in the chain novel.

A computer, too, can communicate through richly textured pictures. Imagine next the law network function projected as a virtual reality. Here, the web of the computer graphics grid is drawn so fine and in so many colors that it reveals itself as the shapes and images of a textured landscape. Audio and tactile output channels are incorporated to accompany the visual display, reflecting the network function's multidimensionality. The virtual landscape is a grand, active, dynamic theory-game world populated with judges and other legal actors who enter into it, experience it, communicate through it, remake it. The virtual landscape might even be imagined as a Gibsonian cyberspace, a lived consensual hallucination (replete with rogue AI denizens?) in which the law is itself the stuff of both intelligences and environment.

As the computer graphics grid-surface finds an analog in the quilt, so the virtual reality finds its analog in a tapestry. The squares of the quilt disap-pear into a seamless fabric. Like the quilt, the tapestry is n-dimensional and is constantly being woven and rewoven by its makers.

The quilt and tapestry metaphors depart considerably from the conven-tional AI picture. They are posed here as examples of how AI metaphors can suggest other, noncomputer metaphors and vice versa. Also, the quilt and tapestry metaphors give us some perspective on the hidden assumptions of the AI metaphors. What *sort* of machine is the law's mind? Not only is it not necessarily a judicial slot machine, but it may even be nothing at all like a computer. It may be a needle and thread, and human hands to work them.

6

Rules and Judgment

Classical, connectionist, and fuzzy AI systems operate for the most part in highly abstract or simplified problem domains. Rodney Brooks criticizes this. He suggests that the very things that we abstract away in these systems are the things that make AI problems hard to begin with.[1] Analogously, the approximations to law that are rules and legal theories may be seen as abstracting away the hard part of the problem—judgment. As we saw earlier, it is human judgment that makes legal rules meaningful. But what is judgment? And to what degree can we understand how we make judgments?

We have considered law's implementation in AI mind-machines and have viewed law itself as an AI mind-machine. Here, we look at law's "implementation" in the human mind-machine and explicitly consider what AI can tell us about human legal reasoning, especially judicial decisionmaking. Like AI systems, human legal actors are called upon to implement indeterminate legal rules. And like AI systems, human actors are called upon to make categorizations and judgments and are limited in their ability to explain those judgments.

Beyond the Law of Rules

It is rare, however, that even the most vague and general text cannot be given some precise principled content—and that indeed is the essence of the judicial craft.
—Justice Antonin Scalia, "The Rule of Law as a Law of Rules" (1989)

Far more important than our commitment to the image of the passive judge is our commitment to the idea that the judge's job in the case before him is to get the right answer.
—Judge William Wayne Justice, "The Origins of *Ruiz v. Estelle*" (1990)

There is a persistent notion that the law is a system of formal rules. On this view, legal rules insofar as possible ought to be hard and fast. Rules are seen as statements of the law, not guides or approximations. They are to be clear, precise, and determinate. They are prior to cases and are to be obeyed, not interpreted. The rule of law should, wherever possible, be the law of rules.[2]

However, the law of rules is a metaphor. To the extent that legal actors speak as though that metaphor were the only one possible, they fundamentally distort the nature of legal rules, of law, and of the relationship between the two. We have seen that law may be viewed, for example, as an embodied artificial intelligence. Rules may be thought of as theory-maps, approximations to the law that receive content only through interpretation. In general, there are many possible metaphors of law and legal rules. As metaphors, they necessarily emphasize some aspects of law and legal rules and de-emphasize or mask others.

Indeterminacies Revisited

Radin lists five assumptions underlying the rule-of-law model: "(1) Law consists of rules; (2) rules are prior to particular cases, more general than particular cases, and applied to particular cases; (3) law is instrumental (the rules are applied to achieve ends); (4) there is a radical separation between government and citizens (there are rule-givers and appliers, *versus* rule-takers and compliers); (5) the person is a rational chooser ordering her affairs instrumentally."[3] Rule-based approaches to classical AI embody parallel assumptions: (1) Knowledge in a discipline can be formalized as rules; (2) rules are prior to particular cases; (3) rules are applied to achieve ends; (4) rules are given by the programmer and not modified by the system; (5) the system models a human expert who is a rational user of rules. The experience of classical AI in general, and legal expert systems in particular, shows that these assumptions, save perhaps (3), are in many if not most cases invalid. The search for new approaches to AI is in part a response to the breakdown of these assumptions. We may expect an analogous breakdown in law.

The five rule indeterminacies explored earlier in the context of legal AI systems apply to human legal actors as well. Indeterminacy is inherent in the nature of legal rules themselves. Moreover, additional indeterminacies arise with human actors. Whereas an AI system takes its rules as a given, human actors may change the rules themselves. As the law evolves in time, new approximations are needed to fit its shape. Conversely, as powerful legal actors pose their preferred approximations, the law may evolve to conform thereto. A legal actor who cannot change a rule but knows that the rule may soon be repealed or modified may interpret the rule differently from the way she would if she expected it to remain in place.

Even supposing that individual legal rules were themselves determinate, the logic by which the rules are applied would not be. Legal logic is only metaphorically formal deductive logic. Certain classical AI legal expert systems, for instance, those based on the technique known as logic programming, are premised on the legal-logic-as-formal-logic metaphor. In considering the viability of such systems, Berman and Hafner note several ways that the metaphor breaks down. They point out that legal logic is nonmonotonic, so that new information added to the system may change prior results. Legal logic employs devices such as legal fictions and maxims that permit conclusions opposite from those that would follow from strict adherence to basic rules. Whereas formal logic permits only one solution to a problem, legal logic presupposes that arguments can be and must be made on both sides of a case. Although many classical AI systems are not restricted to formal logic, Berman and Hafner's example is instructive. Between the indeterminacies of the substantive rules and the indeterminacies of legal reasoning, it is unrealistic to expect that a system of legal rules can as a general matter be made to behave deterministically.[4]

Rules and Human Reason

For the most part, lawyers and judges do not reason through legal rules. They may cite rules, and they may engage in practice that after the fact could be characterized as conforming to the rules, but they do not ordinarily follow a step-by-step, rule-by-rule thought process. In some instances, a substantive rule may become incorporated as an automatic part of a lawyer's routine. Even in situations where legal rules are invoked explicitly, as in legal arguments and judicial opinions, the application of the rules is, as lawyers are fond of saying, a matter of interpretation. Knowing how to apply a legal rule in context is a craft. It is part of what is meant by knowing how to think like a lawyer. Although the substantive rules of law can straightforwardly be written down, the rules for thinking like a lawyer cannot be, if they can be written down at all.

In analyzing the issues of a case at bar, a purely rule-based approach might begin by asking which rules of a known set of rules could possibly apply to the case, and then considering the scope of applicability of each rule in turn. Such would be the approach of a classical rule-based expert system. In contrast, a human attorney tends to see rule-issue pairs all at once, as complete patterns. In the purely rule-based approach, the rules are supposed to decide the case. Again, a rule-based expert system operates this way, and that is one of its chief limitations. In contrast, the experienced human attorney knows when and how to go beyond the rules. Unlike the expert system, the human can understand the scope of any given rule and can abstract from the full complexity of a real-world problem those aspects to which the rule may be applied. Furthermore, the human can adapt to situations in which the legal rules are nascent, unsettled, or essentially vague.

Rules frame the issues and nonissues in a case. In legal argument and in judicial opinions, discussion of the choice of available rules and of the rules' scope of applicability is limited to a fairly narrow range. Rules set the agenda for discussion; it can be difficult even to see the potential issues that are hidden away in the assumptions behind the rules, much less to build arguments on them. But critical jurisprudences teach that a case may be decided as much by these hidden potential issues, by the questions that are never asked, as by the disposition of issues that are raised. A rule-based expert system must accept the framing of issues provided by its designer. A human attorney, though, can recognize and challenge the framing, bringing to light the hidden assumptions of the law and offering alternatives, at least in scholarship if not always in the courts. The attorney can understand how community and cultural norms, the state of the law and legal ideology, and a court's particular ideology and politics, as well as traditional policy, equity, and due process concerns, all play into the case, and how justice may best be served by not letting the rules decide the case.

Why Rules Matter

Saying that lawyers invoke, interpret, transcend, communicate through, and frame legal discourse with rules may seem to contradict the notion that lawyers for the most part do not reason through rules. The contradiction is illusory, however. Rules matter.

Rules matter first of all because the distinction between reasoning that explicitly considers rules and reasoning that is more or less automatic is not sharp. A lawyer may draw on a range of thought styles in doing any given task, moving fluidly between rule-oriented and expert reasoning and using these in combination.[5] He is likely to be involved in an ongoing learning process, constantly incorporating new rules into his practice and formulating new rules from that practice. A lawyer or student learning a new area of law relies on rules as learning tools, using them to develop a base of proficiency from which he later can develop the kind of expertise that permits seemingly instinctual responses to complex situations. The link between rule-oriented and expert reasoning is a link between theory and practice. A discussion of the psychology of that link is beyond the scope of this essay, but it seems safe to say that it is real and significant.

Rules also matter because the distinction between substantive legal rules and the "rules" for thinking like a lawyer is likewise not sharp. The ability to interpret substantive legal rules cannot be radically divorced from the content of those rules. The knowledge of how to apply legal rules in context, although generalizable to some degree across areas of law, ultimately depends on the rules themselves. This is perhaps particularly apparent in a specialty like tax law, but it is true in all branches of law. In particular, the lawyer's ability to cope with rules' open texture depends in part on his understanding of the clear cases. One must understand the core before one can extend to the penumbra.

Thus, the seeming contradiction arises only on a particular, formalist conception of rules. If one assumes that rules are things that one uses by chunking along through them, step by step, and if one assumes that the rules through which one chunks are the substantive legal rules, and if one assumes further that this is the only thing to do with rules, then one may ask how it can be that we use rules for so many purposes yet "for the most part do not think through rules." In fact, we do use rules and use them other than in a formalist way. With a nonformalist conception of rules, no paradox arises. Indeed, the previous two paragraphs' implicit distinction between rules as a process of thought (the rule-oriented reasoning versus expert reasoning dichotomy) and rules as the substance of that thought process (the rules versus interpretation dichotomy) loses its meaning. Even the dichotomy between rules as objects of thought and the person as the subject doing the thinking dissolves. Classical rule-based expert systems embody the formalist conception of rules, including the sharp process-substance and thinker-thought (subject-object) dichotomies. The limits of such systems serve as a reminder of the limits of these dichotomies as well as of the formalist rules. The formalist conception of rules may be a useful metaphor for purposes of discussion, but it should not be confused with what human beings actually do.

As rules matter, so too does our view of what rules are. A change from one prevailing view of rules to another may affect norms, strategies, and attitudes regarding how rules should be interpreted. A student who is taught that legal rules are formal rules may be more comfortable with the notion that rules are to be followed than is a student who is taught that legal rules are theory-games, for whom that notion may make little sense. At the same time, the student taught that rules are games may find it easier to see beyond the explicit issues raised by the rules. In general, as Radin suggests, a change in our view of rules may affect our view of "our roles as legal actors," and that may have "subtle but pervasive consequences" for practice.[6]

The Law of Connections

At the most general level, our metaphor of law matters. What we mean by the rule of law, and our beliefs about how best to achieve it, may change if we allow ourselves to see the rule of law as something other than the law of rules.

We might speculate, for instance, on the meaning of the rule of law as the law of connections. The law of rules suggests that the appropriate model for legal change is the promulgation of new rules. The law of connections suggests a more decentralized, distributed control scheme. The behavior of individual legal actors gives rise to the emergent properties of the law network. The traditional notion of the states as laboratories might be supplemented by a focus on ways of improving transfer of successful programs between states and of improving regional coordination among states without necessarily resorting to reliance on federal government as a central information clearinghouse.

Likewise, consider the meaning of the rule of law as the law of socially embodied intelligence. This metaphor suggests, among other things, an activist model of judging. Where law's mind is seen as residing in a central brain, judges, as nodes in the network of that mind, are at best connected to each other but are not directly connected to the social body. But if there is no radical mind-body separation, and law is distributed throughout society's body, then each judge is embodied in society. Brain and body, law and society, all are one, and the traditional notion of the judge as a disembodied, passive observer no longer fits. Instead, the judge may seek to ensure that particular cases are brought and may even step off the bench to work with political, social service, and law enforcement institutions in order to improve the justice system as a whole.[7]

More generally, the socially embodied intelligence metaphor suggests that perhaps the key to social-legal reform is to change the body, not just the mind, or better, not to draw a radical distinction between the two. This means focusing on changing behavior together with thought, institutions together with stated norms, society together with law. It suggests that courts, as well as legislatures, act to bring about social change coordinated with legal change. It suggests that legal academics be active in community work and political work, and that they require their students to do the same by integrating such work into the law-school curriculum. In the area of social reform legislation, it may suggest an emphasis on small, community-based pilot and model programs on an equal basis with changes to code provisions and programs run by centralized administrative agencies. Indeed, in its strongest version, not drawing a radical body-mind distinction requires that social-legal change itself be seen as an ongoing process of the entire law-society system, rather than as a series of discrete reforms driven by particular modifications to the law or promulgated by autonomous legal actors. Perhaps this is the rule of law as the law of interactions.

It is not suggested that the alternative metaphors presented here are better than the law-of-rules metaphor. Clearly, the separation of law and society, the separation of powers, and the ideal of the passive rule-following judge serve critically important purposes, in particular the purpose of constraining the exercise of naked power by opportunistic individuals. The alternative metaphors likewise embody constraints, but the time-tested checks on power provided by the law of rules are not to be lightly discarded. Law that engages in too-active social engineering raises the specter of totalitarianism.[8] Rather, the point here is that new metaphors of law can lead to an increased awareness of alternatives for the legal system. The alternatives may or may not be ones that would have been thought of otherwise and may or may not prove viable. In the end, it does not matter. The key is to shake up thinking, to get out of habitual patterns of problem solving. The legal system will be more effective when its actors contemplate a greater range of choices.

Good Uses for Clear Rules

Although any rule must be interpreted, there is nonetheless such a thing as a clear legal rule: It is a rule that most people in a given legal culture would interpret the same way under most circumstances. Many legal rules, especially statutes, regulations, and well-settled common law are of this kind. Indeed, a criticism of all jurisprudences that question the validity of the notion of clear rules is that such jurisprudences focus on the hard cases. Conventional wisdom holds that something like 95 percent of all lawsuits filed are settled, and something like 95 percent of all potential lawsuits are never filed. If there were no such thing as clear rules of the sort defined here, the legal system might well grind to a halt.

The rule that there shall be two senators per state is a very clear rule. So is a rule that there shall be no cocaine sold in the park. The rule that there shall be no vehicles in the park is also a clear rule, most of the time. Similarly, the mailbox rule for contract offer and acceptance has become clear, most of the time, because the hard cases have for the most part long since been litigated. Even the essentially vague rule that persons shall be entitled to due process is clear in the vast majority of cases.

To the extent that rules can be made clear, all other things being equal, they probably should be. The question is whether and when all other things are equal. The goal of clear rules is an important ideal, but it is equally important not to let that ideal become entrenched dogma, valued for its own sake. Clear rules are no guarantee of justice. They may in fact work against justice, as when they are overbroad, insufficiently sensitive to different subcultures, or malevolent. (Consider the railroad car segregation rule at issue in *Plessy v. Ferguson*.)[9] They may also not always be the best available approximations to the law. Courts have long recognized that in highly context-sensitive situations, the abstraction inherent in any rule may bring about more harm than good, and that standards, balancing tests, or case-by-case evaluations may be more appropriate.

Following is a short catalog of some of the ways that rules may be helpful. The list given here is intended to be illustrative, not exhaustive. The rules contemplated in the list may derive from the written law, from practical know-how, or from legal theory.

Rules may helpfully be used—

1. To formalize legal doctrine so that it may be *communicated*. In particular,
   * To permit ease of discussion. In particular, a single rule, such as the rule against perpetuities, may become a shorthand for an entire body of knowledge.
   * To provide a framework around which to *organize* legal analysis.
   * To serve as a *checklist* or mnemonic device for practicing attorneys or law students. Consider hornbooks and treatises and proof-of-facts encyclopedias in this regard. Similarly, consider a law-school course outline or a practitioner's outline. The rules remind the lawyer or student what to do, ensuring thoroughness and consistency in work product.
   * To begin the process of educating students in a theory or discipline, so that they may develop a base of proficiency.
2. To *simplify* and make more predictable a body of legal doctrine previously in disarray. Here, the rule drives the doctrine rather than the reverse. On the view that law is a connectionist network, a legislature's or high court's promulgation of rules may create or simplify the structure of the network function or may represent the selection of one branch of a bifurcated or multivalued function. The legislature or court

says, "The law is approximately thus" and leaves it up to the network to compute the exact value.

3. To elucidate *inconsistencies* and ambiguities in doctrine and between conflicting doctrines. In particular, construction of a legal expert system tends to foster this process.

4. To create and clarify *expectations* among legal actors and in society at large. In particular,

   - To *restrain* the opportunistic exercise of individual power by shaping appropriate attitudes among legal actors. Traditionally, a clear rule is seen as a path, a straight and narrow road to follow; it is seen as authority to be obeyed. These metaphors imply a subservience to a greater good. Such subservience becomes part of the psychology of legal actors and, if not unreflective, constitutes an important component of an overall commitment to do justice.

   - To give official *sanction* or authority to particular social conduct or norms.

   - Conversely, to *stigmatize* and thereby discourage certain conduct. It is easy to think of ways for a government to use stigmatizing rules to repress dissent or to discriminate against certain social groups, but stigma can also play a positive role, at least in certain instances. Arguably, for instance, society as a whole is made better off by codifying certain violent crimes.

5. To serve as a *cross-check* on judicial reasoning. A judge's written opinion is analogous to the debriefing of an expert prior to the construction of an expert system. The judge is forced to formalize in rules what cannot be entirely formalized; in the process, the judge may become aware of flaws or hidden assumptions in his or her expert practice, and specifically, of ways in which that expert practice does not apply to the case at bar.

6. To permit *predictability* in planning-oriented legal tasks.[10] In drafting a will or a contract, the practicing lawyer wants to know where the law is well-settled and where it is not, and to steer clear of the places where it is not. Attorneys use boilerplate contracts and form wills as starting points because such documents are known to work. More generally, rules set forth the core of an area of law, enabling the planner to stay away from the penumbra. This saves clients time and money.

7. To permit *construction of legal AI systems* for practical task automation in suitably narrow problem domains.

Explanation and Justification

(Scene I. Cindy is three years old. She is waiting at the table for dinner.)

MOM: We'll have dinner in five minutes, Cindy.

CINDY *(rising intonation)*: Why?

MOM: Because the hot dogs will be finished cooking then.

CINDY *(same intonation, more insistently)*: Why?

MOM: Because they only take . . .

CINDY *(interrupting Mom, singing)*: A B C D F G I . . . Why?

* * *

(Scene II. About seven minutes later. Mom and Cindy are eating—or at least Mom is. Mom has a glass of water. Cindy sees a drinking straw on the table near Mom's glass.)

CINDY *(points to the straw)*: Look Mommy, look look look Mommy Mommy. Use the straw Mommy. Use the straw. Use the straw Mommy. Use the straw.

MOM: No, I don't want to.

CINDY *(you guessed it)*: Why?

MOM: Because I like to drink water right from my glass.

CINDY: Why?

MOM *(with a mix of infinite patience and utter exasperation)*: Because.

CINDY: Why? WHY WHY WHY WHY WHY WHY?[11]

It is often desirable that an AI system be able to explain how it has reached its conclusions. Such explanation capability enables a human being to second-guess the system's judgment. It may also be useful for a programmer debugging or improving the system. To be helpful, the system's explanation must capture relevant information in sufficient detail and present it in a way responsive to the needs of the person requesting the explanation. Unfortunately, that is not always possible.

Connectionist AI is sometimes criticized on the grounds that connectionist systems generally do not provide explanation capability. Indeed, lack of explanation seems inherent in connectionist approaches. A connectionist network matches patterns at the level of the network, with no single node or connection's behavior determining the outcome of the match. Classical AI is more suited to providing explanations, after a fashion. A rule-based expert system, for example, can be built to keep track of each rule it considers, and on request to list out the key decisions leading to its ultimate conclusion.

This sort of explanation permits a programmer to identify and, if necessary, modify a particular rule where the system seems to be making poor choices. However, a rule-by-rule listing says nothing about the motivations or assumptions behind the rules. Moreover, the rule listing can go only so far; at some point, the computer's response to "Why did you do that?" is likely to be, "Because you asked me to."[12]

Cindy unreasonably demands an explanation for everything. Her own explanations are likewise unreasonable. Asked to explain why she has done something she knows she was not supposed to do, she says, in a rising-and-then-falling whine, "Because I HAD to." Of course, Cindy knows that under the circumstances, her parents' questions are for the most part rhetorical.[13] Still, her response is instructive. Human beings, like computers, may sometimes be unable to explain their motivations and may be unable to explain themselves beyond a certain point.

In many cases, it is not explanation but justification that is wanted. An explanation tells how a decision or judgment was reached; a justification tells why it was reached. An explanation reveals task structure; a justification reveals agent psychology. The explanation-justification dichotomy is not sharp, but it may nonetheless be useful for purposes of discussion.[14] Humans, like connectionist systems and unlike classical systems, may be unable to give principled, step-by-step accounts of their thought processes. But humans, unlike most connectionist systems and like certain classical systems, may be able to provide justifications that show the context or the bases of their conclusions.[15]

Privileged Access

People sometimes make assertions about mental events to which they may have no access and these assertions may bear little resemblance to the actual events.
—Richard Nisbett and Timothy Wilson,
"Telling More Than We Can Know" (1977)

It is often said that a computer has no idea of what it is doing. Certainly, the computer has no subjective sense of self-awareness, either of its decisionmaking or of its subsequent explanations or justifications. However, even subjective self-awareness is no guarantee of knowing how or why one behaves as one does. In their famous article "Telling More Than We Can Know," research psychologists Nisbett and Wilson show in a series of experiments that subjects are often unaware of the factors that influence their choices or behaviors. Nisbett and Wilson propose that when asked to give the reasons for their behavior, subjects reconstruct rather than retrace their thought processes, basing their reconstructions on internal theories or models of their own behavior. Where the theories are inaccurate or inapplicable, the subjects' explanations tend to be incorrect.[16] Nisbett and Wilson challenge the traditional notion that people have privileged access to their own thought processes; that is, that through introspection, people can know more than outside observers about how they make their decisions.

Nisbett and Wilson's conclusions are controversial. They acknowledge that their experimental methodology is subject to limitations. Furthermore, it is not clear to what degree and in what situations their experimental findings generalize to real life.[17] Nisbett and Wilson emphasize that their studies do not demonstrate "that people *could never* be accurate about the processes involved [in their decisionmaking or behavior]. . . . What the studies do indicate is that such introspective access as may exist is not sufficient to produce accurate reports about the role of critical stimuli in response to questions asked a few minutes or seconds after the stimuli have been processed and a response produced."[18] Even to the extent that Nisbett and Wilson are correct in asserting that people reconstruct behavior from internal theories, their experiments probe only the limits of those theories. Nisbett and Wilson acknowledge that our theories of self work well much of the time, and that we do have a great deal of privileged knowledge. Notwithstanding these caveats, "Telling More Than We Can Know" is widely believed and often cited. To the degree that Nisbett and Wilson's findings are correct and are applicable outside of the laboratory, human explanation capability is inherently limited.[19]

Coherence

Even if we disregard the limits suggested by Nisbett and Wilson, it is apparent that the human mind is subject to only a limited degree of self-probing. If we suppose that one knows the influences on one's behavior, and that one's self-theories are accurate and applicable, it is still not possible to explain how one's thought processes work beyond a certain point, at least if the sort of explanation that one is trying to give is a mechanistic one. This is seen in the phenomenon of an expert's being unable to quite put into words how she handles a problem, but it appears as well in everyday life. Consider for instance the process of reading this paragraph. How do you do it? You read the words and interpret them; but how do you do that? You know the letters and words because you were taught them and have practiced them. But how is it that the words call to mind certain ideas? And how is it that you can selectively focus your attention on the paragraph and maintain a train of thought that enables you to place each sentence in context? At some point, explanation is not forthcoming. Another example:

What is your mother's maiden name? Now, *how* did you recall that? "It just came to me." A final example: How did you wake up this morning? Not how did you get out of bed (although if you tried to explain how you kept your balance and so forth, you might be stymied), but mentally, how did you go from sleep to wakefulness? One moment, you were dreaming, or even wholly unconscious; shortly thereafter, you were *you* again. How did it happen? "I don't know, it just did." And why did you do it at the time and in the way you did? "Because my alarm went off. I had to go to work." All right, but *why* did you engage in that particular mental process and not some other? "Why? I don't know. Because I had to."[20]

Demands for a mechanistic sort of explanation are no more sensible than Cindy's incessant WHYs. It makes little sense to ask how one performs mental processes that occur without conscious volition. It also seems to make little sense to ask for explanations of mental processes that occur on time scales of under one second, the sorts of processes modeled in connectionist AI. It is unclear that we have any access to such processes beyond knowing their results. There is a flash of recognition, a recall of a memory, an instant of sensation, but we cannot say how we bring these things about.

What we can do, though, is describe the cluster of thoughts and images that go through our minds. In extended reasoning processes, occurring on time scales of more than one second,[21] we are aware of a series, or perhaps a whirlwind, of intermediate impressions and thoughts. Those thoughts may be intermediate results in a longer chain of reasoning, alternative formulations of the final result,[22] or even seemingly unconnected to the reasoning. They may seem to move in many directions simultaneously. They may or may not capture important aspects of the reasoning process.[23] But in any case, our description of such thoughts may be the sort of explanation capability—or perhaps we should say, justification capability—that makes sense.

We may expect, if nothing else, that a person's intermediate thoughts will be connected to and coherent with her overall thought process. Just as rules are important in legal reasoning even though people do not for the most part reason through rules, conscious thoughts and impressions are presumably important in extended reasoning even though they may not be the mechanism of such reasoning. More generally, we may expect a person's thoughts to cohere with one another.[24] Fleck's description of what it is like to give "an accurate historical account of a scientific discipline" might well apply to the human mind: "It is as if we wanted to record in writing the natural course of an excited conversation among several persons all speaking simultaneously among themselves and each clamoring to make himself heard, yet which nevertheless permitted a consensus to crystallize."[25]

The kind of explanation or justification that is helpful, then, paints a picture of the patterns of coherence of a person's thoughts. Explanations and justifications for beliefs and actions appear plausible in part because they are consistent with other beliefs and actions.[26] A simple example illustrates. Suppose you are asked to describe the following picture:

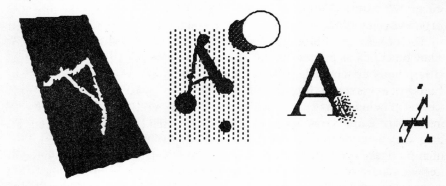

FIGURE 2

These are letter *A*'s, but all have been altered in one way or another. You recognize as much virtually without thinking about it. You cannot explain, mechanistically, how it is that you classified these as *A*'s, or how you knew there were four, or that they were all capital *A*'s, and so forth. Nor can you say how you filtered out the balloons accompanying the second *A* from the left. But if asked, for instance, how you know that the third item from the left is an *A* you might reply, "Well, it's true that part of the lower right side is missing, and appears to have been spray-painted over. Still, I'm sure it's an *A* because it has two legs that converge to a point at the top, and a crossbar about halfway down." This sort of explanation or justification, in this case a description of the whole in terms of parts and subparts, comes about purely after the fact. You probably recognized the *A* all at once and only later dissected it into parts. You are an expert at letter recognition, and articulation of your expert knowledge is something distinct from using it. Still, the justification does show that your beliefs about the picture are coherent. The same features (the two converging legs and the crossbar halfway down) that enabled you to confirm your classification of the third item from the left apply equally well to the other three items. Other sorts of after-the-fact coherence justifications give further support to your conclusion. For example, if asked for additional reasons you think that the picture is a picture of *A*'s, you might reply, "Well, this is supposed to be a simple example, so it's likely to consist of familiar shapes or patterns, and this document was probably prepared on a word processor, so a graphic based on a letter would be fairly easy to incorporate," and so forth.[27]

By analogy, much more complex pattern categorizations, beliefs, judgments, and the like may similarly be justified after the fact in terms of coherent beliefs. As in the simple case, the whole-parts or constituent-belief coherence justification is one possibility; the discussion of context or background assumptions, another; and many others might be imagined as well.

The coherence of an individual's thoughts bears a metaphorical resemblance, as well as perhaps a constitutive relationship, to the sociocultural or disciplinary conceptual coherence associated with a Kuhnian paradigm. A pattern categorization (or belief or judgment) and its justification in terms of coherent beliefs may be seen as a gestalt, and a flip in that gestalt may, in a reversal of Kuhn's own metaphor, be seen as a paradigm shift. This picture suggests that coherence will flip under circumstances analogous to those that prefigure a paradigm shift. A justification may be incomplete and may reflect greater or lesser degrees of coherence; still, when sufficiently strong anomalies arise, coherence will break down and re-form. The metaphor of individual coherence as paradigm coherence also suggests that an individual's coherence pattern may tend to become entrenched despite the presence of anomalies. This is consistent with Gilbert Harman's observation that when an individual's initial belief gives rise to a subsequent belief, and the initial belief is later proved to be false, the subsequent belief may nevertheless persist. Finally, as noted earlier, the flip of a coherence pattern is associated with therapeutic breakthrough and may be marked by a moment of clarity, insight, or laughter.[28]

Introspection

To explain or justify a decision, we must first recall the thoughts and memories that cohere with that decision. For other than simple matters, this requires an ability to introspect. Traditionally, introspection is seen as straightforward and unproblematic. Our intuitions tell us that we know ourselves best. However, we are sometimes very aware of the limits of our introspection. For instance, we may feel there is a pattern staring us in the face but we can't quite put it together. Perhaps when making an important personal decision, we may go to a close friend who we feel knows us in some sense better than we know ourselves. We may consult a therapist or speak with someone in the clergy. We talk it out and get different perspectives.

Similarly, everyday experience, as well as theories of psychological repression and denial, suggest that memories may not always be accessible at will. We may feel as though a memory slips away from our grasp or is stuck and cannot be retrieved. We may believe that we have no memory of a situation or even be unaware the situation ever took place, only to discover later that we do and it did. We may be able to access certain memories only via particular cognitive or sensory modalities. For instance, there are times when we are asked to remember something and cannot, but when asked to close our eyes and imagine it, the memory appears. A long-forgotten smell may trigger memories that dialogue or images do not bring forth.

Given these limits on our ability to introspect, plus those suggested by Nisbett and Wilson, it seems reasonable to ask whether introspective ability can be improved. Traditionally, it is assumed that access to the mind is direct and can be improved through practice and training. This assumption underlies much of psychotherapy. Nisbett and Wilson suggest that at least in some cases, introspection is more a process of reconstruction than recall and is mediated by theories of self. While Nisbett and Wilson leave open the question of whether people can deliberately improve their introspective abilities, they do suggest that self-theories are learned, implying the possibility that such theories might also be relearned.

The picture of therapy suggested earlier, in which a therapist helps the patient to develop a more accurate or helpful theory of self and world, provides a model for improvement of introspective ability that appears to fit both the direct access and the mediated access accounts of introspection.[29] To the extent that the patient has direct access, the patient may reconnect with hitherto repressed or unremembered yet critically important thoughts, feelings, and memories. To the extent that the patient's access is mediated by theory, the therapist guides the patient in developing improved theories that permit the patient to perceive the coherence in what had previously seemed to be an incomprehensible swirl of thought. Direct and theory-mediated access reinforce one another. As new patterns of coherence emerge, so do new memories and feelings, and vice versa.

We usually speak of introspection as though it were a form of perception. We describe thoughts, feelings, and memories as objects, as though they were sense data, and think of ourselves as the subject-recipients of that data. But the *Gedanken* in which the self is gradually stripped away layer by layer suggests that a different view is possible. If we *are* our thoughts and feelings, our memories and motivations, then perhaps introspection is the wrong word. Rather than looking in at ourselves, we are attempting to reinvent ourselves, to reaccess and reassemble the stuff of mind in new ways.

Principled Judgment

I want to urge that there is all the difference in the world between an opponent who has the fundamental intellectual virtues of open-mindedness, respect for reason, and self-criticism, and one who does not; between an opponent who has an impressive and pertinent store of factual knowledge, and one who does not; between an opponent who merely gives vent to his feelings and fantasies (which is all people commonly do in what passes for political discussion), and one who reasons carefully.
—Hilary Putnam, *Reason, Truth, and History* (1981)

A longstanding argument in American jurisprudence concerns whether judges make principled decisions. In crude outline, one side of the argument has it that judges should and do base their decisions on foundational rules and precedents; the other side says that judges make essentially political or idiosyncratic decisions, justifying decisions after the fact with whatever precedents fit. Implicit in this argument is the idea that principled judging is more or less a form of reasoned deduction. The judge who follows the rules reaches the correct conclusion. The judge who makes an intuitive decision and then justifies it after the fact is unprincipled.

Judgment is yet another open-textured or perhaps essentially vague concept. We have trouble saying just what it is, and equal trouble saying how we do it. It has something to do with categorization, but there is much more to it. It may be that judgment is quintessentially that element of legal reasoning that we cannot explain.[30] However, we can and must justify it.

Judgment is at least in part an expert, automatic sort of reasoning that is not well modeled by rule-by-rule deduction. If we recall the mind-machine metaphor, it may be that key aspects of judgment are better modeled by a connectionist pattern match than by a classical rule-based approach; this is suggested by Judge Hutcheson's notion of the judicial hunch. Hunch formation would take place on time scales of under one second and would be impossible to explain in terms of intermediate results, although the resulting hunch could be justified in terms of coherence. However, rules clearly figure into some judgments in the same way they do in legal reasoning generally. Just as connectionist and classical AI model different aspects of intelligence, and both aspects would be necessary in an intelligent machine, so we may expect that both pattern matching and rule-oriented reasoning are aspects of judgment, and that human judges use both, and more.

A judicial opinion is a type of explanation or justification. As such, it ought not be expected to be a mechanistic description of the judge's reasoning process but rather a description of the judge's coherence pattern. Thus a judge who uses a hunch as the basis for an opinion can still be principled so long as "principled" is not taken in a formalist sense. To be sure, the judge's reasoning process is important. A judge should be open-minded, self-critical, and in general make a conscious attempt to reason carefully. Writing the opinion provides the judge with an opportunity to be reflective, to reconsider and go beyond the initial hunch. But the judge's reasoning process need not be a process of deriving decisions from foundational rules and precedents in order to lead consistently to just results and to promote the rule of law, if not the law of rules.

On occasion a judge who attempts to write an opinion that holds according to her initial hunch may find that "the opinion won't write." Faced with a rule or precedent that runs contrary to her hunch, the judge changes or even reverses her holding. This may be seen as an example of coherence flipping. On this view, the judge alters her opinion not because the rule of its own force demands that she do so but because the rule creates a strong anomaly that leads her to reinterpret the entire pattern before her in a new, more coherent way. The judge's coherence pattern need not stand or fall as a whole, and a certain degree of inconsistency or anomaly need not cause the judge to change her mind. But when one or more anomalies cannot be convincingly denied or discounted in the written opinion, and inclusion of the anomalies renders the resulting opinion incoherent or disingenuous, the judge may be led to alter her judgment. At the same time, what counts as incoherent or disingenuous depends in part on the individual judge. One judge's anomalies may be another's exemplars, as is seen in cases where the dissenting and majority opinions seem to be talking past one another.

A judge writing an opinion is subject to the same limits on introspection as anyone attempting to provide an explanation or justification. A judge's inadequate or inappropriate self-theories, or psychological barriers to memory, may limit her ability to know her own motivations in deciding a case. A judge, like a psychotherapy patient, should be able to improve her introspective ability. The idea that judges ought to become more self-aware is not new. Scholars from Jerome Frank to Steven Winter have called for more self-aware judges. The reason is clear: The judge who has a better self-awareness—whether direct or mediated—is likely to make better, more just decisions.

Perhaps judgment seems mysterious and inexplicable, and not well-suited to introspective exegesis, at least in part because judges traditionally are seen as detached, disembodied observer-decisionmakers—in other words, because they are seen in terms of the usual mind-machine metaphor. A judge's decisionmaking process is seen as wholly internal to the judge, and therefore as hidden from and inaccessible to outside observation, perhaps even by the judge herself. If, however, judges are instead seen in terms of an interactionist AI metaphor, a different picture emerges. The focus shifts from judgment to judging, from discrete problem-solving moment to ongoing, situated, improvised process. The new, unaccustomed metaphor invites self-critical judges to examine and verbalize the unspoken components of what they do, and to entertain the notion that little things that ordinarily go unnoticed in their routines may in fact represent significant aspects of the intelligence of the judging process. The interactionist judge might look at the mental or written notes she makes to herself, the way she scrutinizes a witness's eyes or responds to a counsel's tone of voice, even the way she sits in her chair or holds her head. This kind of reflection on practice, although not altogether unrelated to traditional introspection, is more akin to Agre's detail studies of everyday life or Donald Schön's studies of the practices of architects and other skilled professionals.[31] Although it does not provide a way to justify judicial decisions, at least it may help to explain some of judicial decisionmaking.

Cindy may someday be a very good judge. She asks the right question, and she seems to have an instinctive grasp of human nature.[32] She needs to work a bit on her ability to articulate her justifications: "Because I HAD to" is not an acceptable reason for fining someone or sending a person to jail. But with a little practice, she should do as well as the rest of us.

7

A Final Word

Metaphorically, law may be seen as an AI system, and jurisprudence, as the study of the computer science of that system. Arguably, the closeness of analogy between AI and law reflects a common set of problems that have to do in part with common approaches to the nature of the human mind. Both AI and law have run into the limits of formalism, and both are experimenting with new strategies for remaking themselves in nonformalist images. Whatever results these strategies may ultimately produce, the experimentation process is bound to shake up the thinking of practitioners in both disciplines.

It is hoped that the law-AI metaphors developed in this essay turn out to be helpful and fun. Any metaphor of law reveals certain aspects of law and hides others. This hiding comes about in part because law is in some respects inconsistent with the metaphor, and in part because there are aspects of law to which the metaphor simply does not draw attention. By revealing new aspects or combinations of aspects of law, new metaphors such as those developed here may enable us to see new possibilities and opportunities for legal change. *Play with them. See what comes up.*

Appendix

Following is a PROLOG implementation of the simple vehicle-in-the-park example of Chapter 3, along with a printout from a test run of this implementation. The program was written in Advanced AI Systems' PROLOG Version M–1.15 and run on a Macintosh SE computer.

```
                           /* PROGRAM */

/*
 *
 * PROLOG implementation of vehicle-in-the-park problem.
 * The facts are stated first, then the rules.
 * Variables are indicated by capital letters, such as
 * V and P. Constants and rules (predicates) are given by
 * word_symbols in lower case.
 *
 */

                            /* FACTS */

/* PROLOG facts are statements of the form "xxx(yyy)," which
 * translates in English as "It is true that yyy is an xxx,"
 * or more simply, "yyy is an xxx." For example, the PROLOG
 * statement "car(honda)" translates as "A Honda is a car."
 */

/* There are two cars and a truck (a Jeep) in our system. */
car(honda).
car(chevrolet).
truck(jeep).

/* The Jeep is a statue (as suggested by Fuller's
 * hypothetical). */
statue(jeep).

/* The cars and trucks are at various locations. */
location(honda,100,300).
location(chevrolet,200,600).
location(jeep,100,300).
```

```
/* There is also a circus elephant. */
elephant(jumbo).
circus_performer(jumbo).
location(jumbo,100,300).

/* And, of course, a park. The park is at location
 * (100,300). */
park(central_park).
location(central_park,100,300).
```

```
                    /* RULES */
```

```
/* PROLOG rules are statements of the form
 *     "xxx(yyy) :- p1(yyy), p2(yyy)"
 * and more complex variations on the same. They translate
 * into English as "It is true that yyy is an xxx if yyy is
 * a p1 and yyy is a p2." The symbol ":-" means "if."
 * For example, the rule "car(V):-truck(V)" translates as
 * "V is a car if V is a truck."
 */
```

```
/* For purposes of this problem, treat trucks as cars. */
car(V):-truck(V).
```

```
/* V is a vehicle in the park if V is a vehicle and V is in
 * the park. */
vehicle_in_the_park(V,P):-vehicle(V),park(P),in_the(V,P).
```

```
/* V is in the park if its location is coextensive with
 * the park's. Assume for simplicity that an object is in
 * the park if it is at exactly the same location as the
 * park. Compare the X and Y coordinates to see. (VX = PX)
 * means "VX equals PX," just as in English.*/
in_the(V,P):-
     location(V,VX,VY),location(P,PX,PY),(VX = PX),(VY = PY).
```

```
/* Define vehicles. A vehicle has a rider. */
vehicle(V):- has_rider(V).
```

```
/* Something has a rider if it has seats and it moves under
 * its own power. */
has_rider(V):- has_seats(V), self_propelled(V).
```

```
/* All cars and some elephants have seats. */
has_seats(V):- car(V).
has_seats(V):- elephant(V), circus_performer(V).
```

```
/* Elephants and cars are self_propelled if they are not
 * statues. The "!,fail" construction is PROLOGese for
 * "not." */
self_propelled(V):- statue(V),!,fail.
self_propelled(V):- car(V).
self_propelled(V):- elephant(V).
```

```
                    /* END OF PROGRAM */
```

```
                    /* TEST RUN */
```

```
/* Printout from a run of the program. The "?-" is PROLOG's
 * prompt for input. First, see what facts the program
 * knows. List all cars: */
```

```
?- car(C).
   C = honda ;
   C = chevrolet ;
   C = jeep ;
   no
```

```
/* PROLOG prints "no" when it cannot find any more cars in
 * the database. Next, ask for trucks, and then for
 * elephants and parks: */
```

```
?- truck(T).
   T = jeep ;
   no
```

```
?- elephant(E).
   E = jumbo ;
   no
```

```
?- park(P).
   P = central_park ;
   no
```

```
/* Now ask about vehicles: */
```

```
?- vehicle(V).
   V = honda ;
   V = chevrolet ;
   V = jumbo ;
   no
```

```
/* PROLOG correctly ignored the statue of the jeep.
 * Finally, ask for vehicles in the park: */

?- vehicle_in_the_park(V,P).
    V = honda, P = central_park ;
    V = jumbo, P = central_park ;
    no
?- quit

                    /* END */
```

Notes

Chapter 1

1. Grey, "What Good Is Legal Pragmatism?" 19, 22.

Chapter 2

1. The family of technologies known as *artificial life* is also sometimes associated with AI and is sometimes defined to include certain AI technologies. A discussion of artificial life is beyond the scope of this essay; Levy, *Artificial Life,* is a nonspecialist's introduction to the field.

2. For the standard story of the fall and rise of connectionism, according to which Minsky and Papert's 1969 book, *Perceptrons,* nearly killed the field, see Rumelhart and McClelland, *Parallel Distributed Processing,* 1: 111–113, 153–159. Minsky and Papert rebut this characterization in their 1988 revised edition.

3. To be slightly more precise, in LISP, information is expressed as atoms, dotted pairs, lists, or lists of lists. More complex data structures such as frames may be formed from these basic structures. To facilitate speedy data access, data structures may be represented via hash coding. COMMON LISP provides directly for a hash table data structure. But generally, hash tables in LISP are equivalent to the computationally slower list structures that they replace. In PROLOG, data is represented as atoms or as first-order logic statements about atoms.

4. The terms "structured information" and "unstructured information" are from Kosko, *Neural Networks and Fuzzy Systems,* 26.

5. An exception is Korf's work on macro operators, e.g., for solving Rubik's cube. Korf, "Macro Operators." Some classical approaches are able to entertain multiple competing hypotheses, either by reasoning along several branches at once or by backtracking when one line of reasoning fails.

6. Rumelhart and McClelland, *Parallel Distributed Processing,* 2: 329.

7. Learning from examples may be further broken down into supervised learning and reinforcement learning. In supervised learning, the network is presented with stimulus-response pairs, i.e., it is told what the correct answers are. In reinforcement learning, the network is presented with stimuli but must generate its own responses. The network is merely told after the fact whether its answers were correct. See Schneider, "Connectionism: Paradigm Shift for Psychology?" 76.

Besides being supervised or unsupervised, connectionist networks may be based on feedforward or feedback. Kosko classifies various connectionist network models according to whether their encoding scheme is supervised or unsupervised and whether their decoding is based primarily on feedforward or feedback. Thus backpropagation models are supervised feedforward models, and Grossberg's adaptive resonance models are unsupervised feedback models. Kosko, *Neural Networks and Fuzzy Systems*, 17 (table).

8. In a supervised learning network, the training set is a series of exemplars chosen by the researcher. In an unsupervised network, the training set is whatever data is input to the network during some initial time period long enough for the network to learn to do something interesting; strictly speaking, though, the training of an unsupervised network never ends because such a network does not have separate learning and response modes.

9. To emphasize this point, expert systems are sometimes called "novice systems." Telephone conversation with Dean Schlobohm, December 26, 1990. Dreyfus and Dreyfus suggest that they be called "competent systems" to emphasize that they perform their tasks "competently, but not expertly," according to Dreyfus and Dreyfus's fivefold taxonomy of skill acquisition in *Mind over Machine*, 117, 121.

10. This term is taken from Dreyfus and Dreyfus, *Mind over Machine*, 7, 11.

11. "A surgeon does not have words for all the ways he cuts, or a chess master for all the patterns he can tell apart and the types of moves he makes in response." Dreyfus, *Being-in-the-World*, 215. The difficulty that experts have in articulating their expert knowledge is a central theme of Dreyfus and Dreyfus, *Mind over Machine*. See also Barnes and Edge, *Science in Context*, 6–7 (knowing-that versus knowing-how is something that verbal formulations of knowledge fail to capture; even as regards knowing-that, it is not possible to get it all down in words); Dreyfus, *Being-in-the-World*, 67 (attributing the distinction between knowing-that versus knowing-how to John Dewey), 230–231 (Heidegger's primordial and positive understandings); Kuhn, *Scientific Revolutions*, 191 (tacit knowledge learned by doing science rather than acquiring rules for doing it), 193–194 (exemplars versus rules). Schön describes how master teachers of skills such as architecture and classical piano develop their own languages to attempt to communicate their unspoken expert knowledge, and how students learn these foreign languages. Schön, *Educating the Reflective Practitioner*, 100–118 (architecture), 175–216 (music); *Reflective Practitioner*, 76–104 (architecture). Note that the dichotomy between rule-oriented and expert thinking is not sharp. See Chapter 6.

12. But see Baum and Haussler, "What Size Net?" for a discussion of networks' abilities to generalize. It is also sometimes said that the designer cannot predict how large the training data set should be, but Rumelhart points out that standard sampling theory can be used to make such a prediction. Conversation with David Rumelhart, November 27, 1990.

13. Judd, *Neural Network Design*, 100–101. The search for theoretical absolutes may be necessary at this stage of research; the theorems are undoubtedly easier to state and to prove than would be more probabilistic theorems. The importance of theoretical limits should be neither overstated nor understated.

14. Judd, for instance, calls connectionist network design a "black art" absent a theory of learning. Ibid., 99. But Weise points out that nature itself relies on hacks in evolving its intelligent systems. Conversation with Daniel Weise, March 21, 1991.

15. For example, in their article "Connectionism and Cognitive Architecture," Fodor and Pylyshyn argue that there are flaws in Rumelhart and McClelland's work (which is true), that classical AI is right and connectionism wrong (which is false), and that classical AI is better supported by the evidence (which misunderstands the two approaches as being mutually exclusive rather than complementary). Chater and Oaksford offer a persuasive rebuttal to these arguments in "Autonomy, Implementation, and Cognitive Architecture."

16. The story of the blind wise men and the elephant serves as a reminder: The king called his six blind wise men and asked them to inspect an elephant. The wise men approached the elephant and began to grope. The first, feeling the trunk, said, "The elephant is like a long snake." The second one felt the animal's flank. "The elephant is like a wall that reaches to the sky." The third caught a hind leg. "The elephant is like the trunk of a tree." The fourth was nearly impaled on the tusks, and cried out, "It is like two sharp swords!" The fifth felt the animal's ear, and said, "No, it is like the leaf of a rubber plant." And the sixth, who felt the elephant's tail, said, "You all are wrong. The elephant is like a wire brush." The king was sighted, and upon hearing these reactions, he ordered that the six wise men be executed.

17. This is not to imply that classical AI researchers have never worked with robots. Winograd's SHRDLU is but one example of such work. See Winograd and Flores, *Understanding Computers and Cognition*, 109–110; Hofstadter, *Gödel, Escher, Bach,* 586–593, 627–632. But the classical AI notions of intelligence have not seen the robot's body as essential to its very conception of knowledge. For a powerful critique of classical AI's dependence on objectivist epistemology, see Lakoff, *Women, Fire, and Dangerous Things*, 338–352 (chap. 19). In the same vein, see Dreyfus and Dreyfus, *Mind over Machine*, 54; however, Dreyfus and Dreyfus's critique is much more loosely written than Lakoff's.

18. Unlike backpropagation network units, neurons in the human brain may have ten thousand connections apiece. The neurons in different parts of the brain have different structures. Human neurons respond not only to synaptic stimuli but also to hormonal or other stimuli. They communicate through frequency-coded action potentials, not through a simple nonlinear function of summed inputs. They fire asynchronously, or in some cases cyclically. Single neurons do not even necessarily operate as single functional units; see Cohen and Wu, "One Neuron, Many Units?" As for the idea that network units might be likened to groups of neurons or to higher-level informational states, critics contend that this analogy should not be made without an explanation of how such groups or informational states might be constructed of real neurons. It should be noted in this regard that brain functions do not necessarily map one-to-one onto brain anatomy, and that various parts of the brain work together in ways not well understood.

19. It might be argued that although a supervised network may obey the hundred-step rule in performance mode, it does not do so in training mode. Although a single training cycle may obey the rule, the number of training cycles required may far exceed that required for effective learning in biological systems. For instance, Gelperin has taught garden slugs to recognize and avoid certain poisoned foods after only *one* training session. Gelperin, "Rapid Food-Aversion Learning." Apparently, we do not yet know what it is about slug neural networks that permits them to learn so quickly.

20. See, e.g., Barlow, "Unsupervised Learning"; Durbin and Rumelhart, "Product Units"; see also Edelman, *Remembered Present*, 58–63 (DARWIN III).

21. Arbib, *Metaphorical Brain 2*, 405.

22. Electronic mail from David Rumelhart, December 6, 1990. Similarly, Dreyfus and Dreyfus assert the need for both holistic similarity recognition and analytic symbol processing in a machine intelligence. Dreyfus and Dreyfus, *Mind over Machine*, 94. And Minsky and Papert state that the two sets of approaches provide "partial and manifestly useful views of a reality of which science is still far from a comprehensive understanding." Minsky and Papert, *Perceptrons*, xv.

23. The system's complexity would have to be of the right sort (whatever *that* might be). Compare Hofstadter's tangled hierarchies in *Gödel, Escher, Bach,* 691–692, 709–710, with Dreyfus and Dreyfus, *Mind over Machine,* 94–97, critiquing Hofstadter, saying that his tangled hierarchies are no improvement over more conventional sorts of formal-logic-based classical approaches.

24. This is not to say that classical or fuzzy AI systems cannot employ metarules or learning algorithms, only that they usually do not. Even where metarules or learning algorithms are employed, the degree of modification that the basic system structure may undergo is typically quite limited. Similarly, in connectionist systems other than those that learn continuously, the system is trained on a series of examples, and the system response acquired during training is not modified during performance. Even in continuous learning systems, fundamental choices such as the number of nodes in the system and the number and geometry of the connections are not changeable, although in a sufficiently complex system, this might or might not prove to be a major limitation. By way of comparison, the importance to learning of analogous changes in adult human brains (neuronal growth, synaptic changes, etc.) is not yet fully understood; current-day connectionist AI proceeds on the assumption that the most important factor in learning is changes in the strengths of connections between neurons rather than changes in the number or geometry of those connections, but this assumption may or may not ultimately prove correct.

25. The fuzzy truck backing-up system is described in Kosko, *Neural Networks and Fuzzy Systems,* 339–362 (chap. 9); the connectionist version on which it is based is Nguyen and Widrow, "Truck Backer-Upper."

26. The analysis-planning framework is McCarty's. McCarty, "Intelligent Legal Information Systems," 267, 287–288; "TAXMAN," 885. See also Gibbons, "Modeling the Legal Information Process," 289 (diagram of attorney's workflow as iterative loop of "understanding" [analysis] and "action" [planning] phases). Although analysis and planning tasks may be most closely associated with particular aspects of practice, they occur in all types of practice. A litigator engages in planning, as when developing trial strategy; likewise, a corporate lawyer engages in analysis and research.

27. The computer-assisted oral-argument practice example appears in Gibbons, "Modeling the Legal Information Process," 293. The automated hornbook example is from Gardner, *Artificial Intelligence Approach,* 191. Gardner also cites the example of a document-drafting system, ibid., 71.

28. AI systems are now in use that aid police and other law enforcement agents in detecting and solving crimes. See "Technology Takes a Byte out of Crime," *San Jose Mercury News,* May 13, 1990, E1.

29. Gibbons, "Modeling the Legal Information Process," 288–289.

30. HYPO is the centerpiece of Ashley's Ph.D. dissertation, "Modelling Legal Argument," for which Edwina Rissland was principal adviser. In more recent work, Rissland and Skalak have integrated HYPO's case-based AI reasoning with a rule-based component in "Combining Case-Based Reasoning." Other researchers have adopted Ashley and Rissland's approach. For example, Lambert and Grunewald apply the approach in an employee discharge case-based AI reasoning system in "LESTER." Some of the limitations of Ashley and Rissland's approach are explored in Mendelson, "Attempted Dimensional Analysis." The need for the programmer to select the dimensions is potentially a major hurdle; Mendelson comments, "Are Ashley's dimensions so difficult

to select properly that only a top expert in the field can do it? In addition, experts will disagree amongst themselves." Ibid., 136. That dimension selection is tricky suggests that Ashley and Rissland's approach, like other classical and connectionist approaches, is fraught with its share of hacks. Incidentally, Ashley and Rissland do not appear to associate themselves with connectionism, and their programming methodology falls squarely within the classical tradition.

31. SCALIR is described in Rose and Belew's "Connectionist and Symbolic Hybrid" and "Legal Information Retrieval." SCALIR may be the only connectionist legal AI system yet developed in the United States. Ibid., 138: "All previous work on AI and Law falls into the symbolic [i.e., classical] category"; Philipps, "Distribution of Damages Through Neural Networks," 990 n. 9 (listing all articles to date on connectionist legal AI).

32. Gardner suggests that legal AI systems provide insights for law on a theoretical level, a substantive level, and a practical level. Gardner, *Artificial Intelligence Approach*, 191; see also ibid., 16 (work on legal AI systems raises new questions for legal theory). Additionally, research on legal AI systems may further the development of computer science, inasmuch as the techniques used in these systems may find application elsewhere. See, e.g., Berman and Hafner, "Obstacles to Logic-Based Models," 193 (issues for logic programming); Kowalski, "Treatment of Negation in Logic Programs for Representing Legislation" (same); McCarty, "Permissions and Obligations" (programming languages for deontic logic); Rose and Belew, "Legal Information Retrieval" (development of hybrid connectionist-classical approaches; development of effective user interface tools for same).

33. McCarty and Sridharan, "Computational Theory of Legal Argument," 1.

34. The "further definition" quotation is from Brown and Streit, "Expert Systems in Tax," 36, as is the notion of using AI to test intersections of current and proposed laws, ibid., 36–37. The structural regularities idea stems from Rose and Belew, "Legal Information Retrieval," 145.

35. The PROLEXS legal clinic expert system does just this. Oskamp, "Knowledge Representation and Legal Expert Systems," 3. Gardner's observation is from *Artificial Intelligence Approach*, 191; Gibbons's, from "Modeling the Legal Information Process," 289–290. See also Berman and Hafner, "Obstacles to Logic-Based Models," 209–210 (suggesting that expert systems that help attorneys construct arguments, though important, "will never supplant the need for human intervention to assess the relevance and weight of the argument"); D'Amato, "Can/Should Computers Replace Judges?" (a Swiftian proposal to automate certain aspects of judging).

36. An old Ray Bradbury short story (whose title, unfortunately, I have forgotten) suggested this idea. In the story, human beings seek to explore Jupiter. They are converted by machine into creatures adapted to the Jovian climate. Humans so converted inevitably fail to come back from their missions. It turns out that they fail to return not because they do not survive but because the experience of being a Jovian is so heavenly that they do not *want* to come back.

37. Edelman rejects an information-processing approach even while giving a blueprint for one, and while using computer simulation in his own work. Edelman, *Remembered Present*, 28–30, 58–63. Likewise, Putnam's *Representation and Reality* may better be seen as remaking rather than rejecting the mind-machine metaphor.

38. Lakoff explores the problems of objectivism in classical AI. Lakoff, *Women, Fire, and Dangerous Things*, 338–352 (chap. 19). He does not see similar problems with

connectionist approaches, ibid., 338. Some of Lakoff's recent work involves topographic maps in the human visual system, which appear to implement certain functions predicted by his cognitive theory. Telephone conversation with George Lakoff, December 1, 1990.

39. See, e.g., Schneider, "Connectionism: Paradigm Shift for Psychology?" Note that David Rumelhart, coauthor of the leading work on connectionism, Rumelhart and McClelland, *Parallel Distributed Processing,* is a professor of psychology.

40. "We're Not Gonna Take It," from the album *Tommy* (MCA Records). © 1969 Fabulous Music, Ltd. Reprinted by kind permission of Pete Townshend and Towser Tunes, Inc.

41. That we may be unconscious of or may fail to recollect much of our experience does not change the basic point made here. Nor does the observation that we may experience ourselves in different ways, as being more or less detached from or immersed in our world. If all our experience were to become unconsciousness and unrecollection, we would cease to experience ourselves in any way at all. (In dreamless sleep perhaps we *do* disappear.)

42. Brooks, "Intelligence Without Reason," 584.

43. Agre coined the term "interactionism." Agre, "Dynamic Structure of Everyday Life," 19–22. The usage of the term here is somewhat different from Agre's usage. To my knowledge, the term is not yet common in the AI literature. In a recent article, Brooks adopted the working term "behavior-based" to describe his robots; however, he noted that "There is no generally accepted term to describe this style of work." Brooks, "Intelligence Without Reason," 571.

44. Brooks, "Intelligence Without Representation," 14.

45. The basic units of computation in the subsumption architecture are augmented finite state machines, which contain simple state machines, registers, and timers. These may be implemented in microprocessors or directly in hardware. Thus, even though Brooks's robots may have numerous on-board microprocessors, the microprocessors are doing very simple things from a software standpoint. Note that "behavior" is a term of art in some of Brooks's writing, e.g., Brooks, "Elephants Don't Play Chess," 7; however, the word is used here in its everyday sense.

46. Communication between the two processes in this example is minimal; the higher-level wandering behavior is coupled with the lower-level collision-avoidance behavior through simple vector summation. See, e.g., Brooks, "Elephants Don't Play Chess," 8.

47. Multiple independent behaviors may take place at any given level. For instance, each of Genghis's six legs independently executes an identical set of low-level behaviors. Higher-level behaviors can override or subsume these to effect coordination among the legs.

48. See Horswill and Brooks, "Situated Vision in a Dynamic World." This work is summarized briefly in Brooks, "Elephants Don't Play Chess," 11–12.

49. Of course, it could also mean that the rate of species evolution increases exponentially as species become more complex, or it could simply be dumb luck.

50. Agre, "Dynamic Structure of Everyday Life," 15.

51. Ibid., 247; see ibid., 234–249 (comparing Agre's work with other AI research).

52. Although in practice Pengi is simulated on a Lisp Machine AI workstation, its logic is simple combinational logic: AND, OR, and NOT gates.

53. Other studies in the same vein as Agre's episode studies include, for example, Lave's studies of how supermarket shoppers use arithmetic, Lave, *Cognition in Practice,*

152–168; and Schön's analyses of teacher-student interactions at architectural school, Schön, *Educating the Reflective Practitioner*, 100–118, and *Reflective Practitioner*, 76–104. See also Rumelhart and McClelland, *Parallel Distributed Processing*, 1: 4–6 (describing how a hand reaches for a coffee cup on a cluttered desk).

54. Agre, "Dynamic Structure of Everyday Life," 134.

55. Brooks flatly rejects being characterized as a connectionist. Brooks, "Intelligence Without Representation," 17–18. Agre, although ultimately not seeing himself as a connectionist, believes there are useful things to be learned from connectionism, such as the importance of restricting AI computations to those that can be realized in biologically plausible hardware. Agre, "Dynamic Structure of Everyday Life," 177; see ibid., 175–188.

56. At some point it perhaps makes sense to describe a system as centralized even though its computational architecture is nominally decentralized. For example, Toto's "map," which is implemented through an active network of simple computational elements, is decentralized when viewed as a collection of elements but arguably is centralized when viewed as a whole.

Chapter 3

1. "Formalism is the project of making law certain by making legal reasoning deductive." Grey, "Holmes and Legal Pragmatism," 822. In his essay on legal formalism, Schauer writes: "At the heart of the word 'formalism,' in many of its numerous uses, lies the concept of decisionmaking according to *rule*." Schauer, "Formalism," 510 (Schauer's italics). Radin unpacks four senses of traditional legal formalism: analytic connection between rules and particulars; deducibility of rules from foundational values; analytic connection between the words in a rule and the things to which they refer; and logical priority of rules to cases such that the applications of a rule and, in particular, of its words, are already present in the rule. Radin, "Reconsidering the Rule of Law," 793–795.

2. Frank's judicial slot machine appears in Frank, *Law and the Modern Mind*, 209; compare with Kuhn's similarly mechanical image of science in Kuhn, *Essential Tension*, 181–182. Philipps draws an analogy between the scales of justice and a connectionist network. Philipps, "Distribution of Damages Through Neural Networks," 990. Winter, "Transcendental Nonsense," 1189, describes the role of the mind-machine metaphor in the marketplace-of-ideas metaphor.

It is interesting that Frank was perhaps the first person to consider incorporating AI technology into law. He made the suggestion in 1949, shortly after the publication of Norbert Wiener's *Cybernetics* (New York: Wiley, 1948). Gardner, *Artificial Intelligence Approach*, 67.

3. The moped example is from Brest, "Misconceived Quest," 211–213. The term "park" also may be ambiguous. Winter, "Upside/Down View," 1885–1889; see ibid., 1895–1900 (social and legal history of parks in the nineteenth and early twentieth centuries), 1904 (a state park that is a beach caused one court considerable consternation). Problems similar to the vehicle-in-the-park problem have arisen in real-life cases. For example, on February 6, 1922, a New York City magistrate ruled that a child's sled was not a "pleasure vehicle" for purposes of a city ordinance prohibiting all but pleasure vehicles on Central Park driveways. "70 Years Ago," *The Recorder* (San Francisco), February 6, 1992.

4. Berman and Hafner, "Obstacles to Logic-Based Models," 185.

5. According to Gardner, *Artificial Intelligence Approach*, 2, 190, the term "open texture" originated with the philosopher Waismann in 1945 and was introduced into legal scholarship by Hart. See Hart, *Concept of Law*, 121, 125. Apparently, the term has caught on in the legal AI community. On the pervasiveness of open texture, see, e.g., Bench-Capon and Sergot, "Toward a Rule Based Representation," 44 ("Open texture may be seen as vagueness plus a machinery for making a decision when one is required"); Berman and Hafner, "Obstacles to Logic-Based Models," 186 (open texture is "pervasive in our legal system"); Winter, "Transcendental Nonsense," 1195, 1196–1197 (indeterminacy of extension); see also Masterman, "Nature of a Paradigm," 79–88 (discussing centrality of reasoning by analogy and by inexact matching as implied by Kuhn; such inexact matching is not logical inferencing, ibid., 85–87); Austin, *How to Do Things with Words*, 143 (the truth or falsity of a seemingly factual statement such as "France is hexagonal" is highly context-dependent); ibid., 148–149 (truth and falsity are ideals and are better seen as dimensions of assessment than as relations or qualities).

6. See Berman and Hafner "Obstacles to Logic-Based Models," 183; ibid., 195–207 (changes in the judiciary and in society); Winter, "Upside/Down View," 1895–1900 (changes in the social meaning of "park" over time); Winter, "Transcendental Nonsense," 1195, 1197 (substantive indeterminacy). This part of the essay assumes that the text of rules remains fixed; Chapter 6 considers what happens when a legislature, court, or agency changes the rules altogether.

7. An example of deliberate indeterminacy is seen in the phrase "original works of authorship" in the copyright statute 17 U.S.C. § 102 (1982). The phrase is purposely left undefined and is intended to incorporate the judicially elaborated standard of the 1909 Copyright Act, which did not define "original." Copyright Law Revision, 94th Cong., 2d Sess., 1976, H. Rept. 1476, 51.

The possibility also exists that a legislative provision will be unclear on account of hasty or inartful drafting. This may be termed inadvertent indeterminacy.

8. See Berman and Hafner, "Obstacles to Logic-Based Models," 183. Other reasons for contradictory rules or conflicting applications of rules include legal fictions, choice of law, substance versus procedure, and conflicting maxims of statutory construction. Ibid., 195–207.

9. Schauer, "Formalism," 514 (pervasive indeterminacy); Bench-Capon and Sergot, "Toward a Rule Based Representation," 43–44, 59.

10. This example is Winter's. He further observes that the core instance of chair is clear because ours is a culture in which people sit in chairs, not on the floor or on stools. Telephone conversation with Steven Winter, December 20, 1990.

11. "Language" (Suzanne Vega, Michael Visceglia). © 1987 WB Music Corp. & Waifersongs Ltd. All rights on behalf of Waifersongs Ltd. administered by WB Music Corp. All rights reserved. Used by permission.

12. The conduit metaphor is discussed in Winter, "Bull Durham," 659–661, and Lakoff and Johnson, *Metaphors We Live By*, 10–12; see also Dreyfus, *Being-in-the-World*, 221 ("Cartesian model of messages sent from one isolated mind to another"). The dance metaphor is inspired in part by metaphors in Winograd and Flores, *Understanding Computers and Cognition*, 64 (conversation as dance), and Lakoff and Johnson, *Metaphors We Live By*, 5 (argument as dance).

13. It is helpful to keep in mind Agre's admonition about context: "The very word 'context' offers us the dangerous invitation to address the 'problem of context' as if there were a single object or homogeneous substance called 'context' to be explained." Agre,

"Dynamic Structure of Everyday Life," 123. Agre makes this point in a discussion of the ways that context can influence reasoning and judgments, but it applies here as well.

14. See, e.g., Austin, *How to Do Things with Words,* 149 (the traditional dichotomy between factual and normative statements is "in need, like so many dichotomies, of elimination"); Wittgenstein, *Philosophical Investigations,* Part 1, § 241 ("It is what human beings *say* that is true and false; and they agree in the *language* they use. That is not agreement in opinions but in form of life") (Wittgenstein's italics). The job-opportunities example is suggested by Winter, "Cognitive Dimension," 2253–2254 (Livia Polanyi).

15. See, e.g., Winter, "Bull Durham," 676 (generative metaphor as productive of change); Matsuda, "Looking to the Bottom," 333 (multiple consciousness).

16. For simplicity, the mythical programming language used here has been kept as close to English as possible. Implementation details such as whether the system represents frames as lists or through hash tables are not considered; although a simple forward-chaining system is described, a backward-chaining system or a mixed search strategy could equally well have been chosen.

17. Rule-based and logic-programming formulations of the vehicle-in-the-park problem are discussed briefly in Berman and Hafner, "Obstacles to Logic-Based Models," 194–196. A simple PROLOG implementation is given in the appendix.

18. In some systems, this rule would be implemented as a pair of rules in order to avoid the "or" construction in the rule precondition. Also, the negation "C has no RELATIVES" might be problematic in some systems, for instance, in pure logic-programming systems.

19. If the rule were encountered again, the precondition would fail because the VEHICLE's RELATIVES slot value would be a list rather than an atom. (Actually, if the system scans the rules in the order listed here, the system will halt before this rule is encountered a second time.)

20. Several years back in *AI Magazine,* Brachman discussed the brittleness of frame systems in "'I Lied About the Trees.'" He posed a memorable hypothetical about a three-legged yellow elephant (the poor creature had jaundice and had lost a leg). The example that follows was inspired by Brachman's article. See also Berman and Hafner, "Obstacles to Logic-Based Models," 188 (baby, toy, and pink elephants).

21. The examples given here have concerned open-textured nouns. Other parts of speech pose even trickier problems for the rule-and-frame system. In particular, relational words like "in" and "on" can be problematic. Whereas a CAR is associated directly with a frame instance, the fact that a particular CAR is in a particular PARK is represented only implicitly through slot values of several frames. Moreover, relational words are extraordinarily context sensitive. For instance, the ambiguity in the streetlight example is as much a problem of interpreting the word "at" as the word "light" in the expression "Make a left at the first light." "At" does not stand alone; "at the first light" is an expression that must be taken as a whole and interpreted in the context of everyday driving and common sense. See also Lakoff, *Women, Fire, and Dangerous Things,* 416–461 (analysis of the word "over").

22. These routines are sometimes called demons. A demon may, for example, check the dimensions of a slot value or compare a slot value with a different slot's value to check for consistency.

23. Perhaps the boldest attempt to push back the problems of formalism in knowledge representation is Cyc, a classical system that employs a huge knowledge base in an

attempt to capture commonsense understanding. See generally Lenat and Guha, *Building Large Knowledge-Based Systems.* Cyc is currently under development at the Microelectronics and Computer Technology Corporation in Austin, Texas. It is too early to tell how successful Cyc will be, but given that the system appears to be founded on classical assumptions about language and meaning, I find ample reason to be skeptical about its prospects.

24. This may, however, not be so. It is also possible to develop legal expert systems without any diminution of one's formalist convictions. Cf. Weizenbaum, *Computer Power and Human Reason,* 116–127 (compulsive computer programmers).

25. Probabilistic reasoning is arguably a step toward making classical AI more flexible, but it does not alter the basic binary approach, at least not as compared with connectionism. Similarly, property inheritance may be said to make a frame in some sense belong to multiple frame classes, but those classes are themselves discrete.

26. See Rumelhart and McClelland, *Parallel Distributed Processing,* 1: 128.

27. Arbib, "Modularity, Schema, and Neurons," 195. See also Putnam, *Representation and Reality,* 104: "There is absolutely no reason to believe that there is one *computational* state that all possible human beings who think that 'there are a lot of cats in the neighborhood' must be in. And if there is not a single *computational* state that they are all in, then there is not likely to be a relevant *neurochemical* state that they are all in either" (Putnam's italics). This is not to say that there is no correlation between brain structure and brain function; indeed, studies of brain-lesioned and neurologically damaged patients suggest otherwise. See generally Sacks, *Man Who Mistook His Wife.* Still, "knowledge may be duplicated in many places [in the brain], and may by no means be uniformly accessible." Brooks, "Intelligence Without Reason," 581 (summarizing McCarthy and Warrington, "Evidence for Modality-Specific Systems").

28. Radin, "Pragmatist and the Feminist," 1708.

Chapter 4

1. Grey presents his two prongs of pragmatist commitment in Grey, "Holmes and Legal Pragmatism," 798. The first of the two Radin quotations is from Radin, "Pragmatist and the Feminist," 1706; the second is from Radin, "Reconsidering the Rule of Law," 807 (citing Putnam). See Radin, "Pragmatist and the Feminist," 1707 (pragmatist commitment to the dissolution of traditional theory-practice dichotomy).

2. Hilary Putnam, comments in the afterword of *USC-90,* 1915.

3. Putnam, *Reason, Truth, and History,* 209–210; Llewellyn, "Some Realism About Realism," 1236–1237. Putnam observes that words like "should," "ought," and "must" have "a built-in orientation towards action. . . . 'I am not out to do what I should' sounds much odder than 'I am not out to be a good man' (and 'I am not out to do what I must' sounds crazy)." *Reason, Truth, and History,* 210. It is not clear whether Putnam's Is and Ought are quite the same as Llewellyn's.

4. This includes Putnam, "The 'Corroboration' of Theories," in Hacking, *Scientific Revolutions,* 69–70. Arguably, Putnam's philosophy ought not to be regarded as pragmatist until his rejection of functionalism in *Reason, Truth, and History.*

5. Cf. Putnam, "Reconsideration of Deweyan Democracy," 1692–1693. Putnam compares scientific theories, for which there is empirical confirmation; religious theories, for which there is none; and existential choice theories, where the actor "may come to feel

afterward that he made the right choice (although he will hardly be able to 'verify' that he did), but there is no guarantee that he will 'know' later whether he did." Ibid., 1693.

6. Another respect in which the term "theory" is open-textured is its scope of reference. A theory may be grand and all-encompassing or may be localized to a particular problem. A theory of justice is of the former sort; a theory of the case at issue, of the latter sort. Cf. Winter, "Bull Durham," 644 (small-t theory).

7. There is, however, a Borges story about a country where the people constructed a map at a one-to-one scale. Such a map would be not unlike a virtual reality. Borges, "Of Exactitude in Science."

8. The actual function constructed by a connectionist network may not be capable of exact expression in terms of a formula.

9. Grey, "What Good Is Legal Pragmatism?" 22.

10. Winter, "Foreword: On Building Houses," 1600; Lakoff and Johnson, *Metaphors We Live By*, 46–47.

11. Winter, "Bull Durham," 678.

12. Kuhn's later writing focuses on these two meanings (paradigm as exemplar and paradigm as worldview, which Kuhn terms "disciplinary matrix"). See, e.g., Kuhn, *Scientific Revolutions*, 182–191. The term *"Weltanschauung"* as applied to philosophies of science appears in Suppe, *Structure of Scientific Theories*, 126 .

13. As one commentator from the *Economist* put it, "It is undeniable that scientists can now predict, control and create natural phenomena much better than ever before. How does a relativist explain that?" "Philosophy of Science," 70. See also Dreyfus, *Being-in-the-World*, 279 (attributing to Kuhn the "strong claim that no lexicon can be true or false of physical reality"). Even Masterman comments that Kuhn fails to appreciate the importance of technological progress as a yardstick of scientific progress. Masterman, "Nature of a Paradigm," 71. Kuhn maintains that he is *not* a radical relativist; he believes that some scientific theories are better than others, and that science progresses toward the better ones. Kuhn, "Reflections on My Critics," 264.

14. Putnam points out that the incommensurability cannot be radical, or else we could not understand the former paradigm or subsume it as a special case of the new one. He appears to adopt this reading of Kuhn for purposes of discussion; it is not entirely clear whether he actually believes that this is the best reading. Putnam, *Reason, Truth, and History*, 114–119.

15. In fact, Kuhn openly acknowledges Fleck's influence, saying he is unsure what he took from Fleck; see Fleck, *Genesis and Development*, viii–ix (Kuhn's foreword). Kuhn called Fleck's book "a brilliant and [still] largely unexploited resource," ibid., x.

16. *Scientific Revolutions* has sold over half a million copies and been translated into 16 languages; see Warsh, "From 'NP' to 'PC.'" "Paradigm" has become part of the language. A NEXIS search for articles written after 1983 and mentioning Thomas Kuhn turned up well over 200 articles, including an article on strategic business planning, Richard Tanner Pascale, "Strategy," *Business Month*, October 1990, 38, and a classical music review, Edward W. Said, "Orchestre de Paris: Carnegie Hall and Avery Fisher Hall, New York," *Nation*, April 10, 1989, 498.

17. Masterman, "Nature of a Paradigm," 67.

18. The gestalt-flip experiment is best understood as a metaphor, a helpful way of thinking about larger changes in perspective. To say that the gestalt flip of the anomalous playing card experiment, Kuhn, *Scientific Revolutions*, 62–64, is really (whatever "really" means) the same as the conceptual change involved in a paradigm shift may be

fallacious, as the cognitive processes involved may or may not be related in the two instances. The science-as-society metaphor is mentioned in Warsh, "From 'NP' to 'PC'" (calling *Scientific Revolutions* "one of the very finest books of the 20th century, a luminous and surprising picture of science as a metaphor for society"). Kuhn speaks of the centrality of metaphor to science, and of change in metaphor to paradigm shift, in his foreword to Fleck, *Genesis and Development*. Kuhn's emphasis on metaphor may be seen as prefiguring Lakoff's. See, e.g., Kuhn, "Reflections on My Critics," 234 (sharing with Masterman "a common conviction of the relevance of philosophy of language and metaphor"), 266–267.

19. Masterman, "Nature of a Paradigm," 60; see also ibid., 87–88 (Kuhn's "protest against the unconscious dishonesty and the swings of bias with which the history of science has been done in scientific textbooks up to now cuts far too deep" to be ignored).

20. See Warsh, "From 'NP' to 'PC.'"

21. Teachout, "Sentimental Metaphors," 553–554. Teachout notes, "It is fashionable among legal scholars today to see a major cultural shift in the winds." He compares legal paradigm shifts to Jonathan Swift's "mighty revolutions in Philosophy" and offers a tongue-in-cheek catalog of such revolutions. Teachout, "The Soul of the Fugue," 1073–1074 nn. 2, 3.

22. Warsh, "From 'NP' to 'PC.'" Kuhn, now a professor at MIT, has "spent much of the last 20 years fleeing from the widespread popularization of his ideas." Ibid.

23. Fleck, *Genesis and Development*, 27: "Once a structurally complete and closed system of opinions consisting of many details and relations has been formed, it offers constant resistance to anything that contradicts it." See also ibid., 27–38 (discussion of "tenacity of viewpoint," ibid., 28, and of denial). Kuhn seems to suggest that the only way a new paradigm can become fully accepted is for the adherents of the old paradigm to die or retire. See Kuhn, *Scientific Revolutions*, 159 ("elderly holdouts").

24. Telephone conversation with Dean Schlobohm, December 26, 1990.

25. Cf. Suppe, *Structure of Scientific Theories*, 637 (Kuhn's attempt in his later work to split the notion of a paradigm into more precise subconcepts gave up "much of what was most distinctive, original, and exciting about his position").

26. The foregoing argument shares antireductionist premises with Lakoff's argument that metaphor is pervasive in language and human cognition. Both arguments may be rejected by persons who disagree with those premises. To hold that in science and philosophy, rigorous, literal language can convey any message that metaphors can and can do so with far greater precision, and that metaphors are best left to writers of fiction and poetry, is in essence to argue for a reductionist approach. Such an approach favors precise definitions and disfavors seemingly imprecise, undefined, holistic concepts. On this reductionist view, metaphors serve primarily to cluster together ideas that can be more clearly seen when teased apart. Similarly, the clustered ideas represented by paradigms are more clearly seen when disaggregated. This is an oversimplification of both Lakoff's and Kuhn's critics' arguments. Still, one who does not think the whole is greater than the sum of the parts in Lakoff's case is probably not likely to think so in Kuhn's.

27. Kuhn's is, at least nominally, a philosophical theory, and, as mentioned earlier, philosophical theories are for the most part interpretive rather than scientific. It is possible that the critics require a more precise fit between Kuhn's theory and history than is reasonable, and in particular, an unrealistically great degree of precision in the definition of inherently indeterminate terms such as theory, paradigm, and normal science. In that case, Kuhn's theory may be no more (or less) interpretive than other philosophical

theories. It may also be that Kuhn's theory is so slippery in its interpretation of the history of science that it is not properly called philosophical.

28. See Masterman, "Nature of a Paradigm," 75 (one cannot distinguish "a single new research line from a total new science" or "multiple-paradigm science from mature single paradigm science" except "by hindsight"); Warsh, "From 'NP' to 'PC'" ("It is almost impossible to pin down exactly what is meant [by the term 'paradigm']—at least in real time").

29. Masterman distinguishes three kinds of preparadigm science: nonparadigm science (prescientific); multiple-paradigm science, including the so-called soft sciences such as psychology, sociology, and computer science; and dual-paradigm science, including the hard sciences at times preceding the crisis that precipitates a paradigm. Masterman, "Nature of a Paradigm," 73–74. Swaine suggests that computer science exhibits multiple paradigms, and that the best software designers can select among them "at will." Swaine, "Case Study in Paradigm Clash," 131.

30. Pattern-breaking procedures may find more general application outside the therapeutic context, for instance, as aids to creativity. One may achieve different results, or the same results more easily, by directing one's attention to an unaccustomed modality of thought. For instance, in writing an essay, if one hits a point where the words do not come easily, it is sometimes useful to try to visualize a picture of what comes next, or even to imagine hearing a famous author or respected mentor speaking the words.

Chapter 5

1. Elliott, "Holmes and Evolution," 139.

2. Grossberg, "Adaptive Pattern Classification I," 123.

3. The description given here of the adaptive resonance model is highly oversimplified. Grossberg develops the model in ibid. and "Adaptive Pattern Classification II" (see especially at p. 188), coining the term "adaptive resonance" in the latter article. Grossberg, "Competitive Learning," provides a good overview of ART and compares ART with backpropagation and other connectionist techniques. Grossberg argues that ART provides a far more biologically plausible model of neural networks than do other models, which he says are only "metaphorical" representations of biological reality, ibid., 26–27. (Grossberg here uses "metaphor" to refer to figurative language; he is apparently unaware of the deeper mind-machine metaphor that structures his own work as well as the work he critiques.) Papers on adaptive resonance models are collected in Grossberg, *Neural Networks and Natural Intelligence*.

4. Although the metaphor developed here is inspired by ART, the metaphorical law network parallels ART only loosely. To my knowledge, no connectionist network yet built remotely approaches the complexity of the metaphorical network envisioned here. The metaphor is not intended as an endorsement of ART or any other AI approach.

5. See Grossberg, "Competitive Learning," 29–31.

6. Cf. Gardner, *Artificial Intelligence Approach,* 22: Rules are "cognitive tools," neither "authoritative statements of law" nor "adequate descriptions of judicial behavior," but rather "useful cognitive constructs, needed to find order in (or impose order upon) an unruly mass of individual decisions." The resolution of the rule-case dichotomy suggested here does not appear to be reflected in current-day legal AI systems, which for the most part maintain a strong rule-case separation. See, e.g., Rissland and Skalak, "Combining

Case-Based Reasoning" (CABARET). Branting and Porter's GREBE system, which strengthens its ability to match new cases to stored precedents by using rules both to elaborate upon given case descriptions by inferring implicit facts and to reformulate terms in the new case descriptions so as better to match terms in the precedents, effectively uses rules to make given cases and precedents appear more general but does not directly treat rules as generalized cases. See Branting and Porter, "Complementary Warrants."

7. Note that there may be multiple temporal dimensions associated with the network function. Besides real time, against which law's evolution is measured, several time dimensions may characterize any given area of law as a salient feature of cases therein (e.g., time between offer and acceptance, time between the beginning of the running of the statute of limitations and the filing of suit, etc.). Moreover, in theorizing about the future of law, or in posing a hypothetical, one speaks in terms of the imaginary evolution of time; to the extent that such theorizing is part of the law, it poses yet another temporal dimension.

8. Other analogies in the science fiction literature would include the world-controlling computer Multivac that appears in some of Asimov's short stories, including "The Last Question," or the artificial intelligence Wintermute in Gibson's novel *Neuromancer*. In the real world, an analogy might be the now-canceled Defense Department Advance Research Projects Agency's Autonomous Land Vehicle project; see "Pentagon Wanted a Smart Truck," *New York Times,* May 30, 1989, late edition, A1.

9. Jurisprudential scholarship that accepts this picture of law may look more like one of Agre's episode studies than like a traditional law review article. An example may be Blecker, "Haven or Hell?"

Chapter 6

1. Brooks, "Intelligence Without Representation," 5. Brooks discusses classical AI here, but because he distinguishes his subsumption architecture approach from connectionism as well, ibid., 17–18, he presumably would make the same argument for any AI approach that does not produce systems capable of interacting directly with the world in all its complexity. See Brooks, "Intelligence Without Reason," 579–580.

2. A strong version of the argument for clear rules appears in Scalia, "Rule of Law as Law of Rules."

3. Radin, "Reconsidering the Rule of Law," 792.

4. Indeed, even if law *were* a formal system of mathematical logic, Gödel's incompleteness theorem would dictate that the truth of some legal propositions would be undecidable within the system. Rogers and Molzon explore this idea and its consequences for legal theory in "Lessons from Mathematics."

5. The distinction between rule-oriented and expert thinking was discussed in Chapter 2. See Dreyfus and Dreyfus, *Mind over Machine,* 16–51 (five levels of skill). Dreyfus and Dreyfus's levels are best seen as points on a continuum rather than as discrete, and as idealizations (or metaphors?) in the sense that an individual would not be expected to be at precisely one level at a time.

6. Radin, "Reconsidering the Rule of Law," 809; see ibid., 809–810.

7. Judge Justice's lecture "Origins of *Ruiz v. Estelle*" provides a remarkable recent example of effective, if controversial, situated activist judging of the sort envisioned here.

Justice's reinterpretation of faithfulness to the rule of law includes an overriding allegiance to the integrity of the judicial process, see ibid., 10–11, in the vein of Radin, "Reconsidering the Rule of Law."

8. It should be kept in mind, however, that the law of rules is not necessarily inconsistent with social engineering or totalitarianism, as seen in the example of Nazi Germany. Cf. Fuller, "Positivism and Fidelity to Law," 658–661.

9. 163 U.S. 537 (1896). The segregation rule may seem clear, but its clarity depends on the implicit assumption that all parties on the train know who belongs to which race. For a discussion of why racial classifications are neither self-evident nor immutable, see Gotanda's critique of the American hypodescent rule of racial classification in "'Our Constitution Is Color-Blind,'" 23–27.

10. Telephone conversation with Dean Schlobohm, December 26, 1990.

11. This scene actually happened, at the home of some friends in Sunset Beach, Hawaii, January 12, 1991. Cindy's name has been changed to protect her mom. One suspects that Cindy's responses could have been produced by a classical AI program. Cf. Weizenbaum, *Computer Power and Human Reason,* 3–8, 188–191 (ELIZA).

12. An example is seen in the explanation capability provided in Winograd's SHRDLU. Hofstadter, *Gödel, Escher, Bach,* 591.

13. Lest the reader doubt this, when I made the mistake of answering one of Cindy's whys with a Cindy-like "Because I HAD to," Cindy pouted. She knew quite well that she was being teased, and she did not appreciate it.

14. The how-why distinction is from Schlobohm and Waterman, "Expert System Estate Planning," 23. The task structure–agent psychology distinction is from Allen Newell and H. A. Simon, *Human Problem Solving* (Englewood Cliffs, N.J.: Prentice-Hall, 1972) by way of Gardner, *Artificial Intelligence Approach,* 2. "Explanation" and "justification" are open-textured terms, and one may of course choose not to adopt the shades of meaning suggested here. See, e.g., Harman, *Change in View,* 66 ("there is no constant relation between [the] notions" of explanation and justification); ibid., 73 ("There are explanations and explanations").

15. Schlobohm and Waterman, "Expert System Estate Planning," provides an example of a classical system with justification capability. Justifications had to be specially designed into the system, an estate-planning legal expert system to be used directly by clients, because simple traceback explanation capability proved inadequate to answer clients' queries to the system as to why, rather than how, it had made certain choices. Ibid., 23. An example of justification in a connectionist system is Thagard's ECHO, discussed in note 28. It is not clear whether or how a distributed connectionist network might be equipped with justification capability.

16. Nisbett and Wilson provide an extensive list of reasons detailing why subjects' explanations may be correct or incorrect. "Telling More Than We Can Know," 251–253. In general, subjects give correct explanations when influential stimuli are available in memory and are plausible causes of the response in light of their self-theories and when few or no plausible but noninfluential factors are available. They give incorrect explanations when the stimuli are unavailable at the time of judgment, so that reconstruction is not possible; when the theories are inaccurate; or when confusing stimuli are available. Availability may vary with the salience of the events at the time of their occurrence, and with the "strength of the network of verbal associations that spontaneously call events to mind." Ibid., 251. More specifically, factors that may interfere with correct explanation

include removal in time of the event from the judgment; mechanics-of-judgment effects, including positional effects, anchoring, serial-order effects, most-recent-judgment effects, and the like; context; nonevents that contribute to judgments; nonverbal behavior that also contributes; and discrepancies in the magnitudes of cause and effect. Ibid., 252.

17. Consider, for example, that experimental subjects' explanations are retrospective rather than contemporaneous; that subjects have no opportunity to test and correct their beliefs, to ask advice, or to incorporate multiple perspectives; and that in experiments where subjects indicate a change in belief in response to experimental stimulus, such change may or may not be permanent. Cf. Lave, *Cognition in Practice*, 143 (to the extent that psychology experiments pose isolated problems rather than real-life context-situated dilemmas, the experiments may say more about the experimenters or the experimental methodology than about the experimental subjects).

18. Nisbett and Wilson, "Telling More Than We Can Know," 246 (Nisbett and Wilson's italics).

19. Brooks, "Intelligence Without Reason," 581–582, suggests additional reasons to suppose that introspection capability is inherently limited. Perceptual illusions, such as optical and time-perception illusions, may cause perceptions not to reflect accurately the phenomena perceived. Moreover, certain findings of neuropsychology, for example on neurologically impaired or brain-lesioned patients, tend to show that knowledge is stored in context-specific ways, that the brain-mind operates through multiple parallel channels of control, and that in the case of so-called split-brain patients (patients whose corpus callosum has been severed), the left side of the brain may fabricate explanations rather than admit that it knows not what the right side is doing. Brooks postulates that these findings have implications for "the ordinary introspection that goes on when our brains are intact." Ibid., 582. See generally Sacks, *Man Who Mistook His Wife* (portraits of neurology patients).

20. Cf. Marr, *Vision*, 24–25 (computational, algorithmic, and hardware levels). Metaphorically, Marr's levels suggest similar levels in the human mind-brain. The computational and algorithmic levels are not to be seen as hard and fast; what is computational for purposes of one discussion may be algorithmic for purposes of another. The division between the algorithmic and hardware levels may be seen as corresponding to the division between mind and brain. Arguably, the arising of a subjective sense of consciousness from the material brain is ultimately mysterious; I am not satisfied with attempts—e.g., Churchland's eliminative materialism, see Churchland, *Neurocomputational Perspective*, 1–22; Churchland, *Matter and Consciousness*, 43–49—to resolve the mind-brain dichotomy.

The classic formulation of the "how did you know *that?*" style of argument appears in Wittgenstein, *Philosophical Investigations*, for example, in Part 1, § 381 ("How do I know that this colour is red?—It would be an answer to say: 'I have learnt English.'").

21. Such extended processes include the serial reasoning processes of classical AI but are by no means limited to such processes.

22. See, e.g., Nisbett and Wilson, "Telling More Than We Can Know," 241 (discussion of subject who imagined a swinging monkey in the swinging-cord experiment). Kekulé's famous dream of a ring of writhing snakes, which led him to discover the structure of the benzene molecule, may be another example.

23. See ibid., 255 (it is important not to confuse intermediate *output* with mental *process*).

24. Cf. Harman, *Change in View,* 29–42 (chap. 4). Harman contrasts what he calls the foundations and coherence models of belief. According to the foundations model, a person's beliefs rest on one another like the bricks in a building; if a foundational belief is changed, all beliefs based thereon must also be changed. According to the coherence model, a person's beliefs mutually support one another, more or less with none being especially privileged. In particular, where an initial belief gives rise to a subsequent belief, and then the first belief is proved to be false, the subsequent belief may nevertheless persist. Harman suggests that although the foundations model is more traditional and may at first seem more reasonable, the coherence model better describes what people actually do.

As used here, the term "coherence" is not intended to refer to "narrative coherence" or to other uses of the term "coherence" in the scholarly literature.

25. Fleck, *Genesis and Development,* 14–15. See also Hilary Putnam, in the afterword of *USC-90,* 1915 (our moral visions hang together "however loosely and with whatever inconsistencies").

26. "Belief," at least in this context, is a loaded word. Churchland, among others, argues that "belief" and "desire" are no more than mere "folk psychology" notions, not especially useful for purposes of philosophical or cognitive science inquiry. Clark offers a persuasive rebuttal in "From Folk Psychology to Naive Psychology." However, it should not be supposed, as Harman sometimes seems to do, that beliefs and desires may best or even necessarily be represented as propositions. Neither should actions necessarily be seen as deliberate, or beliefs as prior to actions. See Dreyfus, *Being-in-the-World,* 57–58, 86.

27. Cf. Rumelhart and McClelland, *Parallel Distributed Processing,* 1: 8 (ink-spot pictures: partially obliterated letters that would be ambiguous if presented by themselves become unambiguous when presented with other partially obliterated letters in the context of words).

28. Additionally, the metaphor of individual coherence as paradigm coherence underlies Paul Thagard's ECHO, a localist connectionist system that simulates certain features of coherence-based justification. ECHO has been used, among other things, to model the paradigm shifts associated with Lavoisier and Darwin, and to model jury decisionmaking in a murder trial; see Thagard, "Explanatory Coherence." In ECHO, network nodes stand for propositions, and justification is expressed in terms of the nodes' propositional meanings and the network's activation pattern. Thagard's use of the terms "explanation" and "justification" is different from this essay's.

29. Presumably, both the direct-access and mediated-access accounts have some validity, but the range of validity of each is unclear. Perhaps direct access applies primarily to feelings and memories, and mediated access primarily to motivations, but this division should be taken with a grain of salt.

30. "Judgments usually seem systematic, but if there is a system underlying them it does not appear to be rule-based, or, if it is, we have no ability to lay our hands on the rules. We simply cannot say how we do it." Gibbons, "Modeling the Legal Information Process," 290. Dewey recounts the old story of the lay judge in India who was told, as regarded giving reasons for his decisions, "Never try to give reasons, for they will usually be wrong." Dewey, "Logical Method and Law," 17; see also David Bloor, "Formal and Informal Thought," 118 (John Stuart Mill's story of similar advice given by Lord Mansfield). Cf. Schön, *Reflective Practitioner,* 182 (seeing similarity without being able to say, "similar with respect to what").

31. The term "reflection on practice" is Schön's. Schön, *Reflective Practitioner*, 61–62. The usage here may differ somewhat from Schön's usage.

32. As mentioned earlier (see note 13), Cindy knows full well when she is being teased. Compare this with Judge Justice's statement, "I have been lied to and I have been told the truth, and I think that I can usually tell the difference," in "Origins of *Ruiz v. Estelle*," 3.

Bibliography

This book assumes that the reader is somewhat familiar with basic AI concepts as well as with American law and jurisprudence. There are a number of good nontechnical introductory articles on AI. Edwina Rissland's excellent review article, "Artificial Intelligence and Law," summarizes for nonspecialists the history of work in legal AI systems and provides a view of where the field is going. Gruner, "Thinking Like a Lawyer," is a good although somewhat hyped introduction to expert systems. An early proposal for legal expert systems is Buchanan and Headrick, "Some Speculation About Artificial Intelligence and Legal Reasoning." For a brief introduction to connectionist systems, see Dyson, "Neural Net Notes." Probably the best-known work on connectionist approaches is Rumelhart and McClelland, *Parallel Distributed Processing;* the first four chapters of volume one are relatively accessible to nonspecialists. Teitelbaum, "Making Everything Perfectly Fuzzy," is a background sketch of Bart Kosko that also introduces the concepts of fuzzy AI. Kosko, *Neural Networks and Fuzzy Systems,* is a comprehensive engineering text on fuzzy systems and their relationship to connectionist systems. Waldrop, "Fast, Cheap, and out of Control," is a brief nonspecialist's introduction to interactionism. Although written primarily for computer scientists, Brooks, "Elephants Don't Play Chess," is a fairly accessible overview of interactionism; it includes descriptions of the various mobile robots developed at the MIT lab. For a discussion of gnat robots and related topics, see Brooks and Flynn, "Fast, Cheap, and out of Control," and Flynn, Brooks, and Tavrow, "Twilight Zones and Cornerstones." Brooks's "Intelligence Without Representation," which might be called an interactionist manifesto, provides the clearest statement of interactionist design philosophy.

Examples of writings on AI and law from the computer scientist's viewpoint are the conference papers collected in the biennial *Proceedings of the International Conference on Artificial Intelligence and Law* as well as those in the two volumes edited by Walter, *Computer Power and Legal Language* and *Computing Power and Legal Reasoning.* Most of these papers have to do with legal expert systems. An example from the practicing attorney's viewpoint is Morrison, "Market Realities of Rule-Based Software." From the legal commentator's viewpoint is A. Johnson-Laird, "Neural Networks: Intellectual Property Nightmare?" Jurisprudential works on law and AI include Elliott, "Holmes and Evolution," Gibbons, "Modelling the Legal Information Process," and Berman and Hafner, "Obstacles to Logic-Based Models." Often, authors writing from the computer scientist's viewpoint discuss the jurisprudential implications as well as the technical results of their work. However, these authors, such as Ashley, "Modelling Legal Argument," McCarty, "TAXMAN," and Susskind, *Expert Systems in Law,* tend to put computer science first and jurisprudence second. Gardner, *Artificial Intelligence Approach,* may be an exception. Solum, "Legal Personhood for Artificial Intelligences," cuts across the legal commentator's and legal theorist's viewpoints and introduces perhaps yet another viewpoint, that of the philosopher of the mind. Solum considers how placing hypothetical AIs in practical legal contexts can inform understandings of the nature of human intelligence and the possibility of machine intelligence.

Examples of legal AI systems relating to different areas of substantive law include the systems described in Ashley, "Modelling Legal Argument" (trade-secret misappropriation); Branting and Porter, "Complementary Warrants" (worker's compensation); Galtung and Mæsel, "Xcite" (Norwegian Citizenship Act of 1950); Gardner, *Artificial Intelligence Approach* (contract offer and acceptance); Lambert and Grunewald, "Quasi-Precedential Domain" (employee discharge); Schlobohm and McCarty, "EPS II" (estate planning); Sergot et al., "British Nationality Act" (British Nationality Act); Kowalski, "Treatment of Negation" (British Nationality Act); and Susskind, *Expert Systems in Law* (British Latent Damage Act, which deals with negligence claims raised in cases where damage is discovered some time after its occurrence). Tax expert systems are catalogued in Brown, "Tax Expert Systems in Industry," and Brown and Streit, "Survey of Tax Expert Systems"; particular tax expert systems are described in McCarty, "TAXMAN"; Rissland and Skalak, "Interpreting Statutory Predicates"; and Sherman, "Expert Systems and ICAI." Blodgett, "Artificial Intelligence Comes of Age," is aimed at a nonspecialist audience and includes discussion of several legal expert systems, including an asbestos tort claims system.

On the debate over the possibility of sentient machines, see the twin articles Searle, "Is the Brain's Mind a Computer Program?" and Churchland and Churchland, "Could a Machine Think?" The Churchlands have the better argument. Speculations on the nature and origins of intelligence—for example, Hofstadter, *Gödel, Escher, Bach*—abound in the literature; Edelman's biologically based theory, *Remembered Present,* is particularly intriguing and sophisticated.

The vehicle-in-the-park problem is posed in Hart, "Separation of Law and Morals," and Fuller, "Positivism and Fidelity to Law." The problem has been discussed frequently in the jurisprudential literature, including the literature on law and AI. It appears, for example, in Berman and Hafner, "Obstacles to Logic-Based Models"; Brest, "Misconceived Quest"; Gardner, *Artificial Intelligence Approach;* Radin, "Reconsidering the Rule of Law"; Schauer, "Formalism"; Twining and Miers, *How to Do Things with Rules;* Winter, "Upside/Down View"; and Winter, "Transcendental Nonsense."

Pragmatism represents one of several important challenges to the mainstream philosophical tradition commonly associated with thinkers such as Descartes and Kant. Murphy, *Pragmatism,* provides an overview. Grey, "Holmes and Legal Pragmatism," serves as an introduction to legal pragmatism, and the *Symposium on the Renaissance of Pragmatism* is a collection of papers on the subject. For other challenges to the mainstream tradition, see, for example, Dreyfus, *Being-in-the-World;* Lakoff, *Women, Fire, and Dangerous Things;* Putnam, *Reason, Truth, and History;* and Wittgenstein, *Philosophical Investigations.*

Paradigms, of course, originate with Kuhn, *Scientific Revolutions.* Scholarly critique of Kuhn, some of it scathing, is found in Barnes and Edge, *Science in Context;* Hacking, *Scientific Revolutions;* and Suppe, *Structure of Scientific Theories.* A more sympathetic critique is Masterman, "Nature of a Paradigm." "Philosophy of Science" is a good popular article giving a historical overview of the philosophy of science, including a brief discussion of Kuhn. Kuhn addresses his critics in the postscript to his second edition of *Scientific Revolutions* and in his essay "Reflections on My Critics." *Essential Tension* is a collection of Kuhn's essays.

******

Abbreviations:
> *ICAIL-87: The First International Conference on Artificial Intelligence and Law: Proceedings of the Conference,* Northeastern University, Boston, Mass., May 27–29, 1987. New York: Association for Computing Machinery, 1987.
>
> *ICAIL-89: The Second International Conference on Artificial Intelligence and Law: Proceedings of the Conference,* University of British Columbia, Vancouver, Canada, June 13–16, 1989. New York: Association for Computing Machinery, 1989.
>
> *USC-90: Symposium on the Renaissance of Pragmatism in American Legal Thought,* University of Southern California, Spring 1990. In *Southern California Law Review* 63 (1990): vii–viii, 1569–1928. [The entire September 1990 issue of the *Southern California Law Review* is devoted to the *Symposium.*]

Agre, Philip E. "The Dynamic Structure of Everyday Life." Ph.D. diss., MIT, 1988. [Available as MIT Artificial Intelligence Laboratory Technical Report No. 1085, 1988.]

Arbib, Michael A. *The Metaphorical Brain 2: Neural Networks and Beyond.* New York: Wiley, 1989.

————. "Modularity, Schemas, and Neurons: A Critique of Fodor." In *Computers, Brains, and Minds: Essays in Cognitive Science,* edited by P. Slezak and W. R. Albury. Dordrecht and Boston: Kluwer Academic, 1989.

Ashley, Kevin D. "Modelling [*sic*] Legal Argument: Reasoning with Cases and Hypotheticals." Ph.D. diss., Department of Computer and Information Science, University of Massachusetts, 1988. [A version of this dissertation has been published as Ashley, Kevin D., *Modeling Legal Argument: Reasoning with Cases and Hypotheticals* (Cambridge, Mass.: MIT Press, 1990).]

Ashley, Kevin D., and Edwina L. Rissland. "A Case-Based Approach to Modeling Legal Expertise." *IEEE Expert,* Fall 1988, 70–77.

————. "Waiting on Weighting: A Symbolic Least Commitment Approach." In *AAAI-88: Proceedings Seventh National Conference on Artificial Intelligence,* American Association for Artificial Intelligence, St. Paul, Minnesota, August 21–26, 1988, vol. 1. San Mateo, Calif.: Morgan Kaufman, 1988.

Asimov, Isaac. *I, Robot.* 1950. Reprint. New York: Bantam, 1991.

Asimov, Isaac. "The Last Question." *Science Fiction Quarterly,* November 1956. [Reprinted in numerous collections of Asimov's short stories, e.g., in Isaac Asimov, *The Complete Stories, Volume 1* (New York: Doubleday, 1990).]

Austin, J. L. *How to Do Things with Words.* 2d ed. Edited by J. O. Urmson and Marina Sbisà. Cambridge, Mass.: Harvard University Press, 1975.

Barlow, H. B. "Unsupervised Learning." *Neural Computation* 1 (1989): 295–311.

Barnes, Barry, and David Edge, eds. *Science in Context: Readings in the Sociology of Science.* Cambridge, Mass.: MIT Press, 1982.

Baum, Eric B., and David Haussler. "What Size Net Gives Valid Generalization?" *Neural Computation* 1 (1989): 151–160.

Bench-Capon, Trevor J. M., and Marek J. Sergot. "Toward a Rule Based Representation of Open Texture in Law." In *Computer Power and Legal Language: The Use of Computational Linguistics, Artificial Intelligence, and Expert Systems in the Law.*

Proceedings of the Second Annual Conference on Law and Technology, University of Houston, June 24–28, 1985, edited by Charles Walter. New York: Quorum Books, 1988.

Berman, Donald, and Carole Hafner. "Obstacles to the Development of the Logic-Based Models of Legal Reasoning." In *Computer Power and Legal Language: The Use of Computational Linguistics, Artificial Intelligence, and Expert Systems in the Law.* Proceedings of the Second Annual Conference on Law and Technology, University of Houston, June 24–28, 1985, edited by Charles Walter. New York: Quorum Books, 1988.

Blecker, Robert. "Haven or Hell? Inside Lorton Central Prison: Experiences of Punishment Justified." *Stanford Law Review* 42 (1990): 1149–1249.

Blodgett, Nancy. "Artificial Intelligence Comes of Age." *American Bar Association Journal,* January 1, 1987, 68–70.

Bloor, David. "Formal and Informal Thought." In *Science in Context: Readings in the Sociology of Science,* edited by Barry Barnes and David Edge. Cambridge, Mass.: MIT Press, 1982.

Borges, Jorge Luis. "Of Exactitude in Science." In *A Universal History of Infamy,* translated by Norman Thomas di Giovanni. New York: E. P. Dutton, 1972.

Brachman, Ronald J. "'I Lied About the Trees,' Or, Defaults and Definitions in Knowledge Representation." *AI Magazine,* Fall 1985, 80–93.

Branting, L. Karl, and Bruce W. Porter. "Rules and Precedents as Complementary Warrants." In *AAAI-91: Proceedings Ninth National Conference on Artificial Intelligence,* American Association for Artificial Intelligence, Boston, Mass., July 14–19, 1991, vol. 1. Menlo Park, Calif.: AAAI Press; Cambridge, Mass.: MIT Press, 1991.

Brest, Paul. "The Misconceived Quest for Original Understanding." *Boston University Law Review* 60 (1980): 204–238.

Brooks, Rodney A. "Achieving Artificial Intelligence Through Building Robots." MIT Artificial Intelligence Laboratory Technical Report No. 899, 1986.

———. "Intelligence Without Representation." MIT Artificial Intelligence Laboratory, no issuing agency or report number, 1987. [Reprinted in *Artificial Intelligence* 47 (1991): 139–160.]

———. "Engineering Approach to Building Complete, Intelligent Beings." In *Intelligent Robots and Computer Vision,* Proceedings of the Conference on Intelligent Robots and Computer Vision, Cambridge, Mass., November 7–11, 1988, edited by David P. Casasent. Bellingham, Wash.: SPIE—The International Society for Optical Engineering, 1989.

———. "A Robot That Walks: Emergent Behaviors from a Carefully Evolved Network." *Neural Computation* 1 (1989): 253–262.

———. "Elephants Don't Play Chess." *Robotics and Autonomous Systems* 6 (1990): 3–15.

———. "Intelligence Without Reason." In *IJCAI-91: Proceedings of the Twelfth International Joint Conference on Artificial Intelligence,* Sydney, Australia, August 24–30, 1991, vol. 1, edited by John Mylopoulos and Ray Reiter. San Mateo, Calif.: Morgan Kaufman, 1991.

Brooks, Rodney A., Jonathan H. Connell, and Peter Ning. "Herbert: A Second Generation

Mobile Robot." MIT Artificial Intelligence Laboratory Technical Report No. 1016, 1988.

Brooks, Rodney A., and Anita M. Flynn. "Fast, Cheap, and out of Control." MIT Artificial Intelligence Laboratory Technical Report No. 1182, 1989.

Brown, Carol E. "Tax Expert Systems in Industry and Accounting." *USC Expert Systems Review,* June 1988, 9–16.

Brown, Carol E., and Irva Kay Streit. "Expert Systems in Tax: Current Systems and Potential for the Future." Paper presented at the Fall 1987 Meeting of the Northwest Accounting Research Group, hosted by Oregon State University and Portland State University, Mt. Hood, Oregon, October 16–17, 1987.

———. "A Survey of Tax Expert Systems." *USC Expert Systems Review,* March 1988, 6–12.

Buchanan, Bruce G., and Thomas E. Headrick. "Some Speculation About Artificial Intelligence and Legal Reasoning." *Stanford Law Review* 23 (1970): 40–62.

Bylinsky, Gene, and Alicia Hills Moore. "America's Hot Young Scientists." *Fortune,* October 8, 1990, 56–69.

Chater, Nick, and Mike Oaksford. "Autonomy, Implementation and Cognitive Architecture: A Reply to Fodor and Pylyshyn." *Cognition* 34 (1990): 93–107.

Churchland, Paul M. *Matter and Consciousness: A Contemporary Introduction to the Philosophy of Mind.* Rev. ed. Cambridge, Mass.: MIT Press, 1988.

———. *A Neurocomputational Perspective: The Nature of Mind and the Structure of Science.* Cambridge, Mass.: MIT Press, 1989.

Churchland, Paul M., and Patricia S. Churchland. "Could a Machine Think?" *Scientific American,* January 1990, 32–37.

Clark, Andy. "From Folk Psychology to Naive Psychology." *Cognitive Science* 11 (1987): 139–154.

Cohen, Larry, and Jain-young Wu. "One Neuron, Many Units?" *Nature* 346 (1990): 108–109.

D'Amato, Anthony. "Can/Should Computers Replace Judges?" *Georgia Law Review* 11 (1977): 1277–1301.

Dewey, John. "Logical Method and Law." *Cornell Law Quarterly* 10 (1924): 17–27.

———. *Experience and Nature.* New York: Norton, 1929.

Dreyfus, Hubert L. *Being-in-the-World: A Commentary on Heidegger's* Being and Time, *Division 1.* Cambridge, Mass.: MIT Press, 1991.

Dreyfus, Hubert L., and Stuart E. Dreyfus. *Mind over Machine: The Power of Human Intuition and Expertise in the Era of the Computer.* New York: Free Press, 1986.

Durbin, Richard, and David E. Rumelhart. "Product Units: A Computationally Plausible Extension to Backpropagation Networks." *Neural Computation* 1 (1989): 133–142.

Dyson, Esther. "Neural Net Notes." *Computer Lawyer,* September 1987, 2–7.

Edelman, Gerald M. *The Remembered Present: A Biological Theory of Consciousness.* New York: Basic Books, 1989.

Elliott, E. Donald. "Holmes and Evolution: Legal Process as Artificial Intelligence." *Journal of Legal Studies* 13 (1984): 113–46.

Fleck, Ludwik. *Genesis and Development of a Scientific Fact.* Translated from the German, 1935. Edited by Thaddeus J. Trenn and Robert K. Merton, with a foreword by Thomas S. Kuhn. Chicago: University of Chicago Press, 1979.

Flynn, Anita M., and Rodney A. Brooks. "Battling Reality." MIT Artificial Intelligence Laboratory Technical Report No. 1148, 1989.

Flynn, Anita M., Rodney A. Brooks, and Lee S. Tavrow. "Twilight Zones and Cornerstones: A Gnat Robot Double Feature." MIT Artificial Intelligence Laboratory Technical Report No. 1126, 1989.

Flynn, Anita M., Rodney A. Brooks, William M. Wells III, and David S. Barrett. "Squirt: The Prototypical Mobile Robot for Autonomous Graduate Students." MIT Artificial Intelligence Laboratory Technical Report No. 1120, 1989.

Fodor, Jerry A., and Zenon W. Pylyshyn. "Connectionism and Cognitive Architecture: A Critical Analysis." *Cognition* 28 (special issue, March-April 1988), 3–71.

Frank, Jerome. *Law and the Modern Mind.* New York: Brentano's 1930.

Fuller, Lon L. "Positivism and Fidelity to Law—A Reply to Professor Hart." *Harvard Law Review* 71 (1958): 630–672.

Galtung, Andreas, and Dag Syvert Mæsel. "Xcite (An Expert System for Naturalization Cases)." In *ICAIL-89.*

Gardner, Anne von der Lieth. *An Artificial Intelligence Approach to Legal Reasoning.* Cambridge, Mass.: MIT Press, 1987.

Gelperin, Alan. "Rapid Food-Aversion Learning by a Terrestrial Mollusk." *Science* 189 (1975): 567–570.

Gibbons, Hugh. "Modeling the Legal Information Process." *Legal Studies Forum* 12 (1988): 285–297.

Gibson, William. *Neuromancer.* New York: Ace Science Fiction, 1984.

Goldberg, Steven. "The Changing Face of Death: Computers, Consciousness, and Nancy Cruzan." *Stanford Law Review* 43 (1991): 659–684.

Gotanda, Neil. "A Critique of 'Our Constitution Is Color-Blind.'" *Stanford Law Review* 44 (1991): 1–68.

Grey, Thomas C. "Holmes and Legal Pragmatism." *Stanford Law Review* 41 (1989): 787–870.

———. "Hear the Other Side: Wallace Stevens and Pragmatist Legal Theory." In *USC-90.*

———. "What Good Is Legal Pragmatism?" Speech given at the University of Virginia Pragmatism Symposium, November 8, 1990.

Grossberg, Steven. "Adaptive Pattern Classification and Universal Recoding, I: Parallel Development and Coding of Neural Feature Detectors." *Biological Cybernetics* 23 (1976): 121–134.

———. "Adaptive Pattern Classification and Universal Recoding, II: Feedback, Expectation, Olfaction, and Illusions." *Biological Cybernetics* 23 (1976): 187–202.

———. "Competitive Learning: From Interactive Activation to Adaptive Resonance." *Cognitive Science* 11 (1987): 23–63. [Reprinted in *Neural Networks and Natural Intelligence,* edited by Steven Grossberg (Cambridge, Mass.: MIT Press, 1988).]

———, ed. *Neural Networks and Natural Intelligence.* Cambridge, Mass.: MIT Press, 1988.

Gruner, Richard. "Thinking Like a Lawyer: Expert Systems for Legal Analysis." *High Technology Law Journal* 1 (1986): 259–328.

Hacking, Ian, ed. *Scientific Revolutions.* Oxford: Oxford University Press, 1981.

Harman, Gilbert. *Change in View: Principles of Reasoning.* Cambridge, Mass.: MIT Press, 1986.

Hart, H. L. A. "Positivism and the Separation of Law and Morals." *Harvard Law Review* 71 (1958): 593–629.

―――. *The Concept of Law.* Oxford: Clarendon Press, 1961.

Hofstadter, Douglas R. *Gödel, Escher, Bach: An Eternal Golden Braid.* New York: Basic Books, 1979.

Horswill, Ian D., and Rodney A. Brooks. "Situated Vision in a Dynamic World: Chasing Objects." In *AAAI-88: Proceedings Seventh National Conference on Artificial Intelligence,* American Association for Artificial Intelligence, St. Paul, Minnesota, August 21–26, 1988, vol. 2. San Mateo, Calif.: Morgan Kaufman, 1988.

Hutcheson, Joseph C., Jr. "The Judgment Intuitive: The Function of the 'Hunch' in Judicial Decisions." *Cornell Law Quarterly* 14 (1929): 274–288.

The First International Conference on Artificial Intelligence and Law: Proceedings of the Conference, Northeastern University, Boston, Mass., May 27–29, 1987. New York: Association for Computing Machinery, 1987.

The Second International Conference on Artificial Intelligence and Law: Proceedings of the Conference, University of British Columbia, Vancouver, Canada, June 13–16, 1989. New York: Association for Computing Machinery, 1989.

Jang, Jyh-Shing R. "Fuzzy Modeling Using Generalized Neural Networks and Kalman Filter Algorithm." In *AAAI-91: Proceedings Ninth National Conference on Artificial Intelligence,* American Association for Artificial Intelligence, Boston, Mass., July 14–19, 1991, vol. 2. Menlo Park, Calif.: AAAI Press; Cambridge, Mass.: MIT Press, 1991.

Johnson-Laird, Andy. "Neural Networks: The Next Intellectual Property Nightmare?" *Computer Lawyer,* March 1990, 7–23.

Johnson-Laird, Philip N. *The Computer and the Mind: An Introduction to Cognitive Science.* Cambridge, Mass.: Harvard University Press, 1988.

Judd, J. Stephen. *Neural Network Design and the Complexity of Learning.* Cambridge, Mass.: MIT Press, 1990.

Justice, William Wayne. "The Origins of *Ruiz v. Estelle.*" *Stanford Law Review* 43 (1990): 1–12.

Kelman, Mark. *A Guide to Critical Legal Studies.* Cambridge, Mass.: Harvard University Press, 1986.

Konner, Melvin. *The Tangled Wing: Biological Constraints on the Human Spirit.* New York: Holt, Rinehart and Winston, 1982.

Korf, R. E. "Learning to Solve Problems by Searching for Macro Operators." Ph.D. diss., Carnegie-Mellon University, 1983. [Available as Carnegie-Mellon University Department of Computer Science Technical Report CMU-CS–83–138, 1983.]

Kosko, Bart. *Neural Networks and Fuzzy Systems: A Dynamical Systems Approach to Machine Intelligence.* Englewood Cliffs, N.J.: Prentice-Hall, 1992.

Kowalski, Robert. "The Treatment of Negation in Logic Programs for Representing Legislation." In *ICAIL-89.*

Kuhn, Thomas S. *The Structure of Scientific Revolutions.* 2d ed. Chicago: University of Chicago Press, 1970.

―――. "Reflections on My Critics." In *Criticism and the Growth of Knowledge.* Proceedings of the International Colloquium in the Philosophy of Science, London, 1965, vol. 4, edited by Imre Lakatos and Alan Musgrave. Cambridge: Cambridge University Press, 1974.

————. *The Essential Tension: Selected Studies in Scientific Tradition and Change.*
Chicago: University of Chicago Press, 1977.

Lachter, Joel, and Thomas G. Bever. "The Relation Between Linguistic Structure and
Associative Theories of Language Learning—A Constructive Critique of Some
Connectionist Learning Models." *Cognition* 28 (special issue, March-April 1988),
195–247.

Lakatos, Imre, and Alan Musgrave, eds. *Criticism and the Growth of Knowledge.*
Proceedings of the International Colloquium in the Philosophy of Science, London,
1965, vol. 4. Cambridge: Cambridge University Press, 1974.

Lakoff, George. *Women, Fire, and Dangerous Things: What Categories Reveal About the
Mind.* Chicago: University of Chicago Press, 1985.

Lakoff, George, and Mark Johnson. *Metaphors We Live By.* Chicago: University of
Chicago Press, 1980.

Lambert, Kenneth A., and Mark H. Grunewald. "LESTER: Using Paradigm Cases in
Quasi-Precedential Legal Domain." In *ICAIL-89.*

Langacker, Ronald W. "Review of *Women, Fire, and Dangerous Things: What Categories
Reveal About the Mind* by George Lakoff." *Language* 64 (1988): 384–395.

Lave, Jean. *Cognition in Practice: Mind, Mathematics, and Culture in Everyday Life.*
Cambridge: Cambridge University Press, 1988.

Leith, Philip. *Formalism in AI and Computer Science.* New York: E. Horwood, 1990.

Lenat, Douglas B., and R. V. Guha. *Building Large Knowledge-Based Systems:
Representation and Inference in the Cyc Project.* Reading, Mass.: Addison-Wesley,
1990.

Levy, Steven. *Artificial Life: The Quest for a New Creation.* New York: Pantheon, 1992.

Llewellyn, Karl. "Some Realism About Realism—Responding to Dean Pound." *Harvard
Law Review* 44 (1931): 1222–1264.

McCarthy, Rosaleen A., and Elizabeth K. Warrington. "Evidence for Modality-Specific
Systems in the Brain." *Nature* 334 (1988): 428–430.

McCarty, L. Thorne. "Reflections on TAXMAN: An Experiment in Artificial
Intelligence and Legal Reasoning." *Harvard Law Review* 90 (1977): 837–893.

————. "Intelligent Legal Information Systems: Problems and Prospects." *Rutgers
Computer and Technology Law Journal* 9 (1983): 265–294.

————. "Permissions and Obligations: An Informal Introduction." In *Automated
Analysis of Legal Texts: Logic, Informatics, Law.* Papers from the Second
International Conference on *Logica, Informatica, Diritto,* Florence, Italy, September
1985, edited by Antonio A. Martino and F. Socci Natali. Amsterdam: North-Holland,
1986. [Also available as Rutgers University Laboratory for Computer Science
Research Technical Report LRP-TR–19, 1986.]

————. "Intelligent Legal Information Systems: An Update." *Law and Computers*
(Japan) 5 (July 1987): 196–202. [Reprinted in *Expert Systems in Law: Impacts on
Legal Theory and Computer Law,* edited by H. Fiedler, F. Haft, and R. Traunmüller
(Tübingen: Attempto, 1988).]

McCarty, L. Thorne, and N. S. Sridharan. "A Computational Theory of Legal
Argument." Rutgers University Laboratory for Computer Science Research Technical
Report LRP-TR–13, 1982.

Marr, David. *Vision: A Computational Investigation into the Human Representation and
Processing of Visual Information.* New York: W. H. Freeman, 1982.

Martin, Anne W. "Expert-Novice Differences and Implications for Choice of Bench Versus Jury Trial." *Cardozo Law Review* 13 (1991): 575–588.

Masterman, Margaret. "The Nature of a Paradigm." In *Criticism and the Growth of Knowledge.* Proceedings of the International Colloquium in the Philosophy of Science, London, 1965, vol. 4, edited by Imre Lakatos and Alan Musgrave. Cambridge: Cambridge University Press, 1974.

Matsuda, Mari J. "Looking to the Bottom: Critical Legal Studies and Reparations." *Harvard Civil Rights and Civil Liberties Law Review* 22 (1987): 323–399.

Mendelson, Simon. "An Attempted Dimensional Analysis of the Law Governing Government Appeals in Criminal Cases." In *ICAIL-89.*

Minsky, Marvin. *The Society of Mind.* New York: Simon and Schuster, 1986.

Minsky, Marvin, and Seymour Papert. *Perceptrons: An Introduction to Computational Geometry.* Expanded ed. Cambridge, Mass.: MIT Press, 1988.

Morrison, Rees W. "Market Realities of Rule-Based Software for Lawyers: Where the Rubber Meets the Road." In *ICAIL-89.*

Murphy, John P. *Pragmatism: From Peirce to Davidson.* Boulder, Colo.: Westview Press, 1990.

Nagel, Thomas. "What Is It Like to Be a Bat?" *Philosophical Review* 83 (1974): 435–450.

Nguyen, D., and B. Widrow. "The Truck Backer-Upper: An Example of Self-Learning in Neural Networks." In *IJCNN-89: Proceedings of the International Joint Conference on Neural Networks,* Institute of Electrical and Electronics Engineers, 1989, vol. 2. San Diego, Calif.: IEEE TAB Neural Network Committee, 1989.

Nisbett, Richard E., and Timothy DeCamp Wilson. "Telling More Than We Can Know: Verbal Reports on Mental Processes." *Psychological Review* 84 (1977): 231–259.

Oskamp, A. "Knowledge Representation and Legal Expert Systems." In *Advanced Topics of Law and Information Technology,* edited by G. P. V. Vandenberghe. Deventer and Boston: Kluwer Law and Taxation, 1989.

Philipps, Lothar. "Distribution of Damages in Car Accidents Through the Use of Neural Networks." *Cardozo Law Review* 13 (1991): 987–1000.

"The Philosophy of Science." *Economist,* April 25, 1987, 70–71.

Pinker, Steven, and Alan Prince. "On Language and Connectionism: Analysis of a Parallel Distributed Processing Model of Language Acquisition." *Cognition* 28 (special issue, March-April 1988), 73–193.

Putnam, Hilary. "The 'Corroboration' of Theories." In *The Philosophy of Karl Popper,* vol. 1, Library of Living Philosophers, vol. 14, edited by Paul A. Schlipp. La Salle, Ill.: Open Court, 1974. [Reprinted in *Scientific Revolutions,* edited by Ian Hacking (Oxford: Oxford University Press, 1981).]

———. *Reason, Truth, and History.* Cambridge: Cambridge University Press, 1981.

———. *Representation and Reality.* Cambridge, Mass.: MIT Press, 1988.

———. "A Reconsideration of Deweyan Democracy." In *USC-90.*

Radin, Margaret Jane. "Reconsidering the Rule of Law." *Boston University Law Review* 69 (1989): 781–819.

———. "The Pragmatist and the Feminist." In *USC-90.*

"Reinventing the Robot." *Economist,* October 27, 1990, 91–92.

Reynolds, Glenn Harlan. "Chaos and the Court." *Columbia Law Review* 91 (1991): 110–117.

Rissland, Edwina L. "Dimension-Based Analysis of Hypotheticals from Supreme Court Oral Argument." In *ICAIL-89.*
———. "Artificial Intelligence and Law: Stepping Stones to a Model of Legal Reasoning." *Yale Law Journal* 99 (1990): 1957–1981.
Rissland, Edwina L., and David B. Skalak. "Case-Based Reasoning in a Rule-Governed Domain." In *Proceedings: The Fifth Conference on Artificial Intelligence Applications,* IEEE Computer Society, Miami, Fla., March 6–10, 1989. Washington, D.C.: IEEE Computer Society Press, 1989.
———. "Interpreting Statutory Predicates." In *ICAIL-89.*
———. "Combining Case-Based Reasoning and Rule-Based Reasoning: A Heuristic Approach." In *IJCAI-89: Proceedings of the Eleventh International Joint Conference on Artificial Intelligence,* Detroit, Mich., August 20–25, 1989, vol. 1, edited by N. S. Sridharan. San Mateo, Calif.: Morgan Kaufman, 1991.
Rogers, John M., and Robert E. Molzon. "Some Lessons About the Law from Self-Referential Problems in Mathematics." *Michigan Law Review* 90 (1992): 992–1022.
Rogoff, Barbara, and Jean Lave, eds. *Everyday Cognition: Its Development in Social Context.* Cambridge, Mass.: Harvard University Press, 1984.
Rorty, Richard. *Consequences of Pragmatism (Essays: 1972–1980).* Minneapolis: University of Minnesota Press, 1982.
———. *Contingency, Irony, and Solidarity.* Cambridge: Cambridge University Press, 1989.
Rose, Daniel E., and Richard K. Belew. "Legal Information Retrieval: A Hybrid Approach." In *ICAIL-89.*
———. "A Connectionist and Symbolic Hybrid for Improving Legal Research." *International Journal of Man-Machine Studies* 35 (1991): 1–33.
Rumelhart, David E., James L. McClelland, and the PDP Research Group. *Parallel Distributed Processing: Explorations in the Microstructure of Cognition.* 2 vols. Cambridge, Mass.: MIT Press, 1986.
Sacks, Harvey, Emanuel A. Schegloff, and Gail Jefferson. "A Simple Systematics for the Organization of Turn-Taking in Conversation." In *Studies in the Organization of Conversational Interaction,* edited by Jim Schenkein. New York: Academic Press, 1978.
Sacks, Oliver. *The Man Who Mistook His Wife for a Hat and Other Clinical Tales.* New York: Summit Books, 1985.
Scalia, Antonin. "The Rule of Law as a Law of Rules." *University of Chicago Law Review* 56 (1989): 1175–1188.
Schauer, Frederick. "Formalism." *Yale Law Journal* 97 (1988): 509–548.
Schlobohm, Dean A., and L. Thorne McCarty. "EPS II: Estate Planning with Proto-types." In *ICAIL-89.*
Schlobohm, Dean A., and Donald A. Waterman. "Explanation for an Expert System That Performs Estate Planning." In *ICAIL-87.*
Schneider, Walter. "Connectionism: Is It a Paradigm Shift for Psychology?" *Behavior Research Methods, Instruments, and Computers* 19 (1987): 73–83.
Schön, Donald A. *The Reflective Practitioner: How Professionals Think in Action.* New York: Basic Books, 1983.
———. *Educating the Reflective Practitioner: Toward a New Design for Teaching and Learning in the Professions.* San Francisco: Jossey-Bass, 1988.

Searle, John. "Is the Brain's Mind a Computer Program?" *Scientific American,* January 1990, 26–31.

Sejnowski, Terrence J., and C. R. Rosenberg. "NETTalk: A Parallel Network That Learns to Read Aloud." Johns Hopkins University Computer Science Department Technical Report JHU/EECS–86/01, 1986.

Sergot, Marek J., F. Sadri, R. A. Kowalski, F. Kriwaczek, P. Hammond, and H. T. Cory. "The British Nationality Act as a Logic Program." *ACM Communications 29* (1986): 370–386.

Sherman, David M. "Expert Systems and ICAI in Tax Law: Killing Two Birds with One AI Stone." In *ICAIL-89.*

Solum, Lawrence B. "Legal Personhood for Artificial Intelligences." *North Carolina Law Review* 70 (1992): 1231–1287.

Spann, Girardeau A. "Secret Rights." *Minnesota Law Review* 71 (1987): 669–722.

Sperber, Dan. *Rethinking Symbolism.* Translated by Alice L. Marton. Cambridge: Cambridge University Press, 1977.

Suppe, Frederick, ed. *The Structure of Scientific Theories.* 2d ed. Proceedings of a symposium on the structure of scientific theories held at the University of Illinois, Urbana, March 26–29, 1969, edited with a critical introduction and afterword by Suppe. Urbana: University of Illinois Press, 1977.

Susskind, Richard E. *Expert Systems in Law: A Jurisprudential Inquiry.* Oxford: Clarendon, 1987.

———. "The Latent Damage System: A Jurisprudential Analysis." In *ICAIL-89.*

Swaine, Michael. "A Case Study in Paradigm Clash." *Dr. Dobb's Journal,* July 1988, 130–137.

Symposium on the Renaissance of Pragmatism in American Legal Thought, University of Southern California, Spring 1990. In *Southern California Law Review* 63 (1990): vii–viii, 1569–1928. [The entire September 1990 issue of the *Southern California Law Review* is devoted to the *Symposium.*]

Teachout, Peter R. [A. Simpleman, Jr., pseud.]. "Sentimental Metaphors." Review of *Lying Down Together: Law, Metaphor, and Theology* by Milner S. Ball. *UCLA Law Review* 34 (1986): 537–576.

———. "The Soul of the Fugue: An Essay on Reading Fuller." *Minnesota Law Review* 70 (1986): 1073–1148.

Teitelbaum, Sheldon. "Making Everything Perfectly Fuzzy." *Los Angeles Times Magazine,* April 1, 1990, 24.

Thagard, Paul. "Explanatory Coherence." *Behavioral and Brain Sciences* 12 (1989): 435–502. Includes commentary by various authors, and Thagard's response to this commentary.

———. "Connectionism and Legal Inference." *Cardozo Law Review* 13 (1991): 1001–1004.

———. "Adversarial Problem Solving: Modeling an Opponent Using Explanatory Coherence." *Cognitive Science* 16 (1992): 123–149.

Tillers, Peter, and David Schum. "A Theory of Preliminary Fact Investigation." *UC Davis Law Review* 24 (1991): 931–1012.

Twining, William, and David Miers. *How to Do Things with Rules: A Primer of Interpretation.* 2d ed. London: Weidenfeld and Nicholson, 1982.

Waldrop, M. Mitchell. "Fast, Cheap, and out of Control." *Science* 248 (1990): 959–961.

Walter, Charles, ed. *Computing Power and Legal Reasoning*. Proceedings of the First Annual Conference on Law and Technology, University of Houston, August 13–22, 1984. St. Paul, Minn.: West, 1985.

————, ed. *Computer Power and Legal Language: The Use of Computational Linguistics, Artificial Intelligence, and Expert Systems in the Law*. Proceedings of the Second Annual Conference on Law and Technology, University of Houston, June 24–28, 1985. New York: Quorum Books, 1988.

Warner, David R., Jr. "The Role of Neural Networks in the Law Machine Development." *Rutgers Computer and Technology Law Journal* 16 (1990): 129–144.

Warsh, David. "From 'NP' to 'PC': The Structure of Differing World Views." *Boston Globe*, December 23, 1990, city edition, A45.

Weizenbaum, Joseph. *Computer Power and Human Reason: From Judgment to Calculation*. New York: W. H. Freeman, 1976.

Winograd, Terry, and Fernando Flores. *Understanding Computers and Cognition: A New Foundation for Design*. Reading, Mass.: Addison-Wesley, 1987.

Winter, Steven L. "The Cognitive Dimension of the *Agon* Between Legal Power and Narrative Meaning." *Michigan Law Review* 87 (1989): 2225–2279.

————. "Transcendental Nonsense, Metaphoric Reasoning, and the Cognitive Stakes for Law." *University of Pennsylvania Law Review* 137 (1989): 1105–1237.

————. "Bull Durham and the Uses of Theory." *Stanford Law Review* 42 (1990): 639–693.

————. "Indeterminacy and Incommensurability in Constitutional Law." *California Law Review* 78 (1990): 1441–1541.

————. "Foreword: On Building Houses." *Texas Law Review* 69 (1991): 1595–1626.

————. "An Upside/Down View of the Countermajoritarian Difficulty." *Texas Law Review* 69 (1991): 1881–1926.

Wittgenstein, Ludwig. *Philosophical Investigations*. 3d ed. Translated by G. E. M. Anscombe. New York: Macmillan, 1958.

Yablon, Charles M. "On the Allocation of Burdens of Proof in Corporate Law: An Essay on Fairness and Fuzzy Sets." *Cardozo Law Review* 13 (1991): 497–518.

Yager, Ronald R. "New Paradigms for Reasoning with Uncertain Information." *Cardozo Law Review* 13 (1991): 1005–1024.

About the Book
and Author

In this provocative essay, Alexander E. Silverman explores the relationship between artificial intelligence (AI) and the law from the point of view of the legal theorist. Beginning with an overview of AI technology, he provides the necessary background review of classical, connectionist, fuzzy, and interactionist approaches to AI, as well as of legal expert systems. He then applies the lessons from this research to a number of jurisprudential topics, including the concepts of indeterminacy, open texture, and essential vagueness; Kuhnian paradigm shifts and the nature of theory; and the production of new metaphors of law. He concludes with a discussion of the lessons of AI research for our understanding of human legal reasoning.

Mind, Machine, and Metaphor is a rich, original, and wide-ranging view of legal theory in the context of AI research. It is essential reading for legal theorists and for legal scholars and students of AI with an interest in each other's fields.

Alexander E. Silverman is an associate with the law firm Townsend and Townsend Khourie and Crew of Palo Alto, California.